THE CAESARS' WIVES

above Suspicion?

By the same author:

THE ONE REMAINS

THE LIFE AND TIMES OF HEROD THE GREAT

THE LATER HERODS

HADRIAN

CAESARS AND SAINTS

THE END OF THE ROMAN WORLD

THE PILGRIM'S COMPANION IN ATHENS

THE PILGRIM'S COMPANION IN JERUSALEM

THE PILGRIM'S COMPANION IN ROME

JERUSALEM

DEATH OF THE ROMAN REPUBLIC

ROME

ROMAN MYTHOLOGY

THE JOURNEYS OF ST PAUL

The Caesars' Wives

above Suspicion?

STEWART PEROWNE

HODDER AND STOUGHTON
LONDON SYDNEY AUCKLAND TORONTO

To V.

Preface

"What dire offence from am'rous causes springs,
What mighty contests rise from trivial things."

SO IT HAS always been in political life: private scandal promotes public crisis. In December of the year 62 BC an assembly of Roman ladies was celebrating the rites of the Good Goddess in the house of a high magistrate of Rome, a praetor, named Julius Caesar, then aged about forty. No males were admitted—even the buckmouse scampered away, a sexual pariah, we are told by a later gossip.

Into this august harem there is reported to have entered in search of Caesar's wife a young lad disguised as a wench. His name was Clodius, and he was already a notorious lecher. He was also the friend of Caesar and the enemy of Cicero, in whose house on the Palatine the rites had been performed in the previous year, that of Cicero's consulate.

That anyone so well known by sight and voice to the upper ranks of Roman society could really have hoped to pass himself off as a female is open to doubt. His *incognita* was soon exposed and he was shown the door. The scandal was all around Rome the next morning. An official enquiry was called for, because besides being a praetor Caesar was also Rome's Chief Priest, which made the alleged profanation doubly impious.

Without waiting for the formal institution of legal proceedings, Caesar dismissed his wife Pompeia on the ground that the wife of the supreme pontiff must be above suspicion.

Was Caesar?

He was as usual heavily in debt. He was about to set out for a provincial governorship in Spain, whither he could not have taken his wife, even if he had wanted to: she was his third and there was one more to come. So why not be rid of her, with Clodius' raffish assistance? When the case was called, Caesar, though cited, refused to give evidence, on the ground that there was no case to state. Clodius relied on an alibi, which Cicero, who had been nagged by his wife into appearing for the prosecution, in vain attempted to demolish. Clodius was acquitted. A crisis ensued which marked the beginning of the end of the Roman Republic.

The facts, the event, have long been forgotten. All that remains is the famous, cynical quip, that Caesar's wife must be above suspicion.

Was she? We shall never know. Were her successors? To the examination of that query this book is dedicated.

Contents

Illustrations

KEY TO ACKNOWLEDGEMENTS

1 Alinari
2 Ashmolean
3 British Museum
4 Corpus Christi College, Cambridge
5 Bibliothèque Nationale, Paris
6 Camera Press, London (photograph by Barnet Saidman)
7 Ny Carlsberg Glyptotek
8 Italian Cultural Institute, London

Introduction

TO STUDENTS OF history, whether they read for pleasure or instruction, no set of men is more familiar than the Roman emperors of the first and second centuries. They are far better known, as a company, and to far more men and women, than the kings of England, France or Spain, and certainly better and more widely than the dynasts of the great empires which preceded theirs, Egypt, Babylon, Persia, Assyria or Macedon.

This familiarity is partly fortuitous; it happens that the surviving chronicles of the first century of our era are more abundant and more detailed than those of any comparable period before the invention of printing. The association of these narratives, either directly or indirectly, with the birth and ministry of Jesus of Nazareth, with the fortunes of the Jewish people into which he was born, and with the rise and first conquests of the Christian faith, confers on them an interest and importance which must for ever remain unique. For the second century, it is true, our documentary sources are lamentably meagre; the imbalance between the earlier and later reigns becomes all too apparent. Fortunately, for the whole epoch with which the present study is concerned, the written word is supplemented by a wealth of illustration. Not only do we possess ar abundance of monuments, in three continents, even in Britain itself, which proclaim with convincing eloquence what manner of men these were; but we may also contemplate literally hundreds of statues of Roman emperors which for vivacity and truth were to remain unparalleled until the early Renaissance—indeed to survey the features of a Medici at Florence is to look at the bust of a Roman emperor.

During the eighteenth century, many a mansion, not only in Italy, but in France, Germany and England as well, was adorned with statues, either original or copied, of the Roman emperors, so that to succeeding generations these men were known not merely as names and symbols but as individuals. Augustus, the grand paradox who founded a monarchy on the neatly bulldozed ruins of a republic, his successor Tiberius whose deputy crucified Jesus of Nazareth, Claudius who invaded Britain, Nero the embodiment of flamboyant wickedness, Titus who destroyed Jerusalem, Trajan who extended the dominion of Rome from the North Sea to the Persian Gulf, Hadrian who left his greatest memorial in northern England, Marcus Aurelius the image of virtue, Caracalla the incarnation of vice, who became emperor at York where his father Septimius had died—these are but a few of the famous gallery. Each one of them is more living, more three-dimensional as it were, than say, William Rufus of England (the earliest known English royal portrait is that of Richard II, in the Wilton Diptych, 1397), Charles V of Spain or Louis XIII of France. Their characters, their deeds, their features even, are part of our mental furniture.

But their wives?

How many of us could name the spouses of even the above famous or notorious ten? How few of us could trace their lives from birth, through marriage and motherhood, or say whether they were good or evil, happy or miserable: or, not least in interest, what influence they had on affairs, that is history? Three or four of these consorts have, it is true, been raised to fame or, more often, damned to infamy. Poppaea, wife of Nero, is the rather unexpected heroine of Monteverdi's masterpiece; Agrippina who with Messalina is generally, if vaguely, accepted as having overstepped every possible margin of error, is post-humously redeemed in one of the greatest dramas ever written—Racine's *Britannicus;* and to play that rôle is still the highest ambition of every débutante in the Salle Richelieu. For the rest, there is no abiding memorial. Then why attempt to describe them? There might indeed be a good case for silence: what is known about them has been told so often before, and what is not known about them now never will be. On the other hand, the wives of the Cæsars, as a company are worth attention, even in an age so remote from them, for several reasons.

The first is that they were a wholly new genus. The 'Roman

matron' had for long been a type recognised in Roman society; but the idea that a single woman should be treated with unique and superior respect was wholly new. Secondly, one has only to scrutinise the list of these exalted ladies to see how many of them there were, which is another way of saying how tenuous was their hold on the affections and position of their lords. Nearly all of them were unhappy women. Above suspicion of one sort or another very few of them were, but it is compassion they excite, not condemnation. Indeed their common epitaph, the general verdict of the society in which they were destined to live, to strive and to die is summed up in de Montherlant's supplication, "*Pitié pour les femmes*".

As is usual with historical investigations of female affairs, the enquiry raises more questions than it answers. In the case of the empresses, two problems arise at the outset. How had an hereditary sovereignty come to be generally accepted, not only in the empire but in Rome itself; and secondly, what really was the moral climate of the court and how far is it typical of the contemporary Roman world? Because it is only in their context that these women can be even approximately estimated. These two questions are tantalising, and have long been so. The paradoxical fact is that the nearer we get to the Romans, the less we understand them. And the difficulties of comprehension lie largely in ourselves. "The eternal landscape of the past" has not changed, but those who descry it have, and still do.

Of the two problems posed above, the former is the more easily resolved. Until quite recently, it was customary in some circles to regard 'ancient Rome' as the ideal republic, the grand democracy, the majestic prototype of all later republics, and this in an era when republics were becoming increasingly popular, in the New World, no less than in the Old. Then came the artful hypocrite Augustus, who by a process of dissimulation and coercion while pretending to restore the republic, erected his own despotism on its ruins. This picture is, to say the least, distorted. For one thing, Augustus did not claim that he had restored the republic: the Latin phrase *res publica* does not mean republic, it means commonwealth, or state. His own words, at the beginning of his *Acts*, as originally set up on bronze tablets before his mausoleum by the Tiber, and known to us from copies, are as follows: "At the age of nineteen on my own initiative and at my own expense, I raised an army by means of which I restored liberty to the commonwealth, which had been oppressed by the tyranny of a faction." Allowing for the natural tendency of an autocrat to speak well of himself, there is much truth in Augustus' claim to be a restorer. It is equally true that there had always inhered in the Roman constitution a strong element of autocracy, quite incompatible with our modern ideas of a 'pure' democracy. Thomas Arnold, who had no higher opinion of Augustus as a man than Edward Gibbon, nevertheless was constrained to write in the final volume of his *History of Rome*: "Whoever has traced the character of the Roman constitution through the successive periods of the Commonwealth, must have observed in it a number of points which are entirely congenial to despotism." This might be accounted strong language for the year 1827; but Arnold makes out a powerful case for his thesis. Consuls, censors, tribunes, even the Senate itself, all exercised arbitrary power. Then there were the special commissions, and most recently the powers conferred on individuals.

Twice had Pompey been invested with sovereign power over a large portion of the empire. . . . When, therefore, that atrocious Commission of Three [generally known as the Second Triumvirate] was instituted in the persons of Augustus, Antonius and Lepidus [in 43 BC] it was a measure not altogether unprecedented. . . . And the imperial power of Augustus was only an enlarged special commission of the same nature. . . . In this manner [Arnold sums up, echoing Gibbon] the government was made gradually to slide into a monarchy, merely by a dexterous application and enlargement of precedents, which had occurred repeatedly through the successive periods of the duration of the Commonwealth.

Once monarchy was established, what more natural than that the monarch should need a sovereign lady to be his consort? Augusta was the natural complement to Augustus.

But why should the fabric be dynastic? This is a far harder query to answer. For from the very beginning it was assumed by the great majority that hereditary it should be. As we shall see, the means by which it became so were makeshift, and in the end fictitious. But the principle was hardly questioned. The only valid reason is to be found in the basis of Augustus' primacy, that is, in a word, the army. In the very opening sentence of his

Acts, already quoted, Augustus says he raised an army. Later in the same document he says that "the number of Roman citizens who bound themselves to me by military oath was 500,000. Of all these I settled in colonies or sent back into their own towns after their term of service something more than 300,000, and to all I assigned lands, or gave money as a reward for military service". This is a suave way of saying that he had created a standing army, and that he had used nicely disguised bribery to maintain its loyalty. At Augustus' death, the regular army numbered twenty-five legions, or about 150,000 men, whose term of service was twenty years. Legionaries were (at this period) forbidden to marry. What was more natural therefore than that the soldiers should regard their 'imperator', their emperor, as their father, and as the fountain of all goodness? And if he was their father, then clearly his own progeny would be his natural successors in that office. As if to reinforce this projection, Augustus enrolled nine or ten cohorts of praetorian guards, of 1,000 each, who served for sixteen years only, and were paid three times as much as the legionaries. They were to be a source of continual strife and division in the years to come; but it was largely on them that Augustus founded his authority, and it would be to his successors that they, no less than the ordinary troops, would look for their livelihood and enrichment. Since the only foreseeably certain method of election is that furnished by heredity, it was of prime importance to the soldiery that this principle should be adopted. And adopted it was. It had a special appeal to Augustus. In the first place it would ensure the continuation of his dynasty (or so he thought, though as we shall see he was doomed to disappointment); and secondly the military basis of his hegemony was decently veiled. So much so that as Tacitus was to point out it was only at the death of Nero in AD 68 that "the grand secret" was publicly revealed.

Thus, with Augustus established as an absolute monarch in all but name, and his claim to be the founder of a dynasty tacitly conceded, nay more, backed by a professional army, all that was now necessary for the completion of the imperial structure was an empress. Augustus was to find an ideal consort, and to acquire her by typically ruthless means. But before we begin the narrative of their joint achievement, it may be well to examine the status of a Roman lady of the day, the advantages she enjoyed, and the difficulties, moral and personal, which she had to combat.

B

As suggested above, morals and morality are largely subjective
a quality which leads those who attempt to improve them liable
to derision or hostility. It is only necessary to contemplate the
English law regarding obscenity to realise this. Unlike other
statutes, which require a jury to establish a fact beyond all
reasonable doubt, in this sole instance the jury is required to
establish a doubt, often uncorroborated by fact. It is not necessary
to prove that one being has depraved or corrupted another:
only that that person has 'tended' to do so.

This tenuity is inherent in morals and judgment on morals.
Shocking as it may appear, the word 'moral' carries, in origin,
no moral sanction whatever. The Latin word *mos*, from which it
is derived, means (to quote the standard work known as *Lewis
and Short*) 'manner, custom, way, usage, practice, fashion, wont,
as determined not by the laws, but by men's will and pleasure'.
The case for Roman morals could not be better put: 'fashion,
determined by will and pleasure'. Fashions change, will is variable,
pleasure manifold. That is why morals are not only fluid, but
have the nature of a stream rather than of a reservoir.

In any consideration of morals, the English-speaking student
turns naturally enough to the Sinaitic tomes of Lecky. Read
today, they have the double advantage not only of casting much
light on Roman morals, but on our own. Lecky, writing a century
ago, saw every light of the spirit through the stained-glass
window of the Judæo-Christian ethic. Now that so many panes of
it have been shattered by vandals from without and redecorators
from within, it is all the more rewarding to read him.

Here are some of his observations on the virtue of the Roman
female from his *History of European Morals from Augustus to Charle-
magne* (1869). Just how reluctant he was to touch the subject
at all is to be inferred from the following caveat: "The virtues
and vices growing out of the relations between the sexes are
difficult to treat in general terms, both on account of the obvious
delicacy of the subject, and also because their natural history
is extremely obscured by special causes." (I.143) When it comes
to marital relations, Rome scores over Greece.

In Greece monogamy had been enforced, though not without
exceptions, but a concurrence of unfavourable influences
prevented any high standard being attained among the men,
and in their case almost every kind of indulgence beyond the

limits of marriage was permitted. In Rome the standard was far higher. Monogamy was firmly established. The ideal of female morality was placed as high as among Christian nations. Among men, however, while unnatural love and adultery were regarded as wrong, simple unchastity before marriage was scarcely considered a fault. In Catholicism marriage is regarded in a twofold light, as a means of propagation of the species, and as a concession to the weakness of humanity, and all other sensual enjoyment is stringently prohibited. (I.104)

In his second volume (p. 297) Lecky has this to say on the rival claims of marriage and virginity, as regarded in Rome:

If we now turn to the Roman civilisation, we shall find that some important advances had been made in the condition of women. The virtue of chastity has, as I have shown, been regarded in two different ways. The utilitarian view, which commonly prevails in countries where a political spirit is more powerful than a religious spirit, regards marriage as the ideal state, and to promote the happiness, sanctity and security of this state is the main object of all its precepts. The mystical view which rests upon the natural feeling of shame, and which, as history proves, has prevailed especially where political sentiment is very low, and religious sentiment very strong, regards virginity as its supreme type, and marriage as simply the most pardonable declension from ideal purity. It is, I think, a very remarkable fact, that at the head of the religious system of Rome we find two sacerdotal bodies which appear respectively to typify these ideas. The Flamens of Jupiter and the Vestal Virgins were the two most sacred orders in Rome. The ministrations of each were believed to be vitally important to the State. Each could officiate only within the walls of Rome. Each was appointed with the most imposing ceremonies. Each was honoured with the most profound reverence. But in one respect they differed. The Vestal was the type of virginity, and her purity was guarded by the most terrific penalties. The Flamen, on the other hand, was the representative of Roman marriage in its strictest and holiest form. He was necessarily married. His marriage was celebrated with the most solemn rites. It could only be dissolved by death. If his wife died, he was degraded from his office.

The Romans were above all practical people. Virginity was an asset, but a material asset. It was a physical condition rather than a virtue. Even so, women must be more virtuous than men. A typically Roman example of this superiority is cited by the elder Pliny, (*Natural History*, xxviii, 23): "It was said that drowned men floated on their backs, and drowned women on their faces; and this, in the opinion of Roman naturalists, was due to the superior purity of the latter."

Roman women, it must always be borne in mind, were far freer than women of other races with whom they came increasingly in contact. Cornelius Nepos, for instance (fl. 50 BC) in the preface of his work comparing Greeks with Romans, remarks on the superior freedom of Roman women, who preside at table. Even today, there are many lands in which no woman would presume to do so. A picture of the Roman matron (the 'big mother', for that is what the Latin word means) is, it is hoped, beginning to assemble itself. But the Latin wife had two competitors. Here again, Lecky is our guide, but in each case he surprises us. First by his attitude to prostitution, which is so much more generous than we should have expected, secondly by the almost clammy state to which the mere notion of homosexual relations reduces him.

Of prostitution he writes (II.283):

Under these circumstances, there has arisen in society a figure which is certainly the most mournful, and in some respects the most awful, upon which the eye of the moralist can dwell. The unhappy being whose very name is a shame to speak; who counterfeits with a cold heart the transports of affection, and submits herself the passive instrument of lust; who is scorned and insulted as the vilest of her sex, and doomed for the most part, to disease and abject wretchedness and an early death, appears in every age as the perpetual symbol of the degradation and sinfulness of man. Herself the supreme type of vice, she is ultimately the most efficient guardian of virtue. But for her, the unchallenged purity of countless happy homes would be polluted and not a few who, in the pride of their untempted chastity, think of her with an indignant shudder, would have known the agony of remorse and despair. On that one degraded and ignoble form are concentrated the passions which might have filled the world with shame. She remains, while creeds and civilisations rise and fall, the eternal priestess of humanity, blasted for the sins of the people.

Most Romans would have agreed with this sacerdotal aspect of prostitution. Indeed many of them were named after their patron goddess Flora (Flusia in Oscan?: cf. modern American *floosy*?) whose festival of flowers was celebrated on the 28th April with a licence which is generally dubbed 'unbridled'. So would Lecky's contemporary, Charles Dickens. If anyone ever upheld 'the unchallenged purity of countless happy homes' (in print) it was he; but he bade his son consult him when he came to London, as to which brothel he might most commodiously frequent. This tolerant attitude to prostitution is not new: Plutarch, in his *Moral Essays*, counsels a newly-married bride to show very much the same indulgence to her husband's periodical lapses; they are to be his sole affair, into which she should not pry.

Roman moralists claimed that homosexuality came to Italy from Greece, which may well be true. Lecky certainly supports that view in the passage in which he is making out a sympathetic case for the Athenian *hetairai*, a class of female companion which even as he was writing in Britain was once again raised into fashion in the Paris of Cora Pearl and La Goulue:

Another cause probably contributed indirectly to the elevation of this class, to which it is extremely difficult to allude in an English book, but which it is impossible altogether to omit, even in the most cursory survey of Greek morals. Irregular female connections were looked upon as ordinary and not disgraceful incidents in the life of a good man, for they were compared with that lower abyss of unnatural love, which was the deepest and strangest taint of Greek civilisation. This vice, which never appears in the writings of Homer and Hesiod, doubtless arose under the influence of the public games, which accustoming men to the contemplation of absolutely nude figures, awoke an unnatural passion, totally remote from all modern feelings, but which in Greece it was regarded as heroic to resist (Plutarch *Agesilaus*, Dio: Laertius, *Life of*

Zeno, Athenaeus xiii, a book of very painful interest in the history of morals).

The popular religion in this, as in other cases, was made to bend to the new vice. Hebe, the cupbearer of the gods, was replaced by Ganymede, and the worst vices of earth were transported to Olympus. Artists sought to reflect the passion in their statues of the Hermaphrodite, of Bacchus, and the more effeminate Apollo; moralists were known to praise it as the bond of friendship, and it was spoken of as the inspiring enthusiasm of the heroic legion of Epaminondas. In general, however, it was stigmatised as unquestionably a vice, but it was treated with a levity we can now hardly conceive. We can scarcely have a better illustration of the extent to which moral ideas and feelings have changed, than the fact that the first two Greeks who were considered worthy of statues by their fellow countrymen are said to have been Harmodius and Aristogeiton, who were united by an impure love, and who were glorified for a political assassination.

"Lilies that fester smell far worse than weeds." Whatever may have been the levity which Athens displayed towards this form of association to which Lecky found it so hard to allude (but nevertheless succeeded in devoting several paragraphs to 'in an English book'), the Romans went in for it with Roman thoroughness, and Roman coarseness. Many a man might foster a passing liking for a handsome youth. Even Virgil, the noblest Roman of them all, is recorded to have loved two lads—Cebes, and Alexander, whom he calls Alexis in the second of his Bucolics. The public baths provided all too easy an opportunity for inspecting the attractions of the golden youth of Rome. Even Saint Augustine has told us in his Confessions how his boorish and tipsy father rejoiced to see his son advancing into manhood as they were bathing together one day.

What made Roman addiction to the custom so unattractive by modern canons was that these unions were not infrequently contracted between two grown men, and so continued. One would be unwilling to credit this, if only on aesthetic grounds, but the evidence is too plentiful and compromising. Sulla, for instance, returned at the end of his days, after marriage—he had five wives—and fatherhood to the creaking embraces of the actor who had been his first lover. Of Julius Caesar it was said that he was every woman's man, and every man's woman, a double taunt recalling his youthful intimacy with King Nicomedes of Cappadocia and his affair with Cleopatra. Caesar was openly unchaste. He didn't mind being called a queen, either. When, after obtaining the governorship of Gaul, he boasted that when it came to the Senate he'd soon be dancing on the members (using the word in a double sense) and someone sneered that that would be difficult for a woman, he jauntily replied that Semiramis had been a queen in Syria, and that the Amazons hadn't done so badly either. Cæsar dressed in an effeminate style, in a tunic with fringed sleeves, and a sloppy sort of girdle (which did not escape Sulla's eyes). Nor towards the end of his life did he hesitate to consign the command of three legions in Egypt to a 'favourite' called Rufio. None of this would be worth recalling but for the striking fact that Caesar's private life (if such it could be called) had absolutely no effect on his troops who, well knowing what manner of man he was—they shouted it out in the streets— adored him to the death. There is other evidence for this quirk in Roman *mores*. Dio Cassius, the Bithynian historian of the second century, puts the reproach into the mouth of Boadicea: "they sleep with boys, and boys past their prime at that," she says. The Spanish-born Martial, in a pretty little sonnet on "What kind of boy I prefer", concludes, "Only to me must he be a boy—to all the rest a grown man."

Being a Roman matron was no sinecure, what with prostitutes and pederasts. Nor were they the only impediments to happy wedlock. Incest was all too common. There is a horrible story told of the emperor Caligula and one of his cronies called Passienus Crispus. Caesar asked him whether he had sexual relations with his own sister, as Caligula had with his. "Not yet," answered Passienus, which was regarded as very proper and prudent, neither accusing the emperor by denying the suggestion nor dishonouring himself by admitting it.

Even Roman regard for chastity was largely hypocritical. The oldest Roman folk-tale concerns a successful rape, that of the Sabines. The famous Lucrece is praised for consenting to be enjoyed by a nobleman rather than have imputed to her intercourse with a slave. Her suicide was incidental, because she had to face death in any case. (Lucrece really owes her fame to the painters of the Renaissance, who found in her an unparalleled opportunity for extolling female virtue while at the same time revealing a maximum area of female flesh.) The most cynical and disgusting aspect of the Roman view of virginity is seen in the rule which forbade the execution of a maiden. When under Tiberius a poor girl was condemned to death for conspiracy, it was ordained that, to preserve the hallowed proprieties, she should first be deflowered by her executioner.

Finally, in the list of humiliations to which the Roman matron was exposed, must be mentioned one which was inherent in the structure of the Roman family itself. This was governed from the very beginning to the end by the *Patria Potestas*, the Paternal Authority. Matrons were lauded, but they had no authority over their children: that resided solely with the father, and to such an extent that, even when a son was grown up, with a family of his own, his father, if still living, had absolute power over him. This power extended to adopted children also, and it could be used with disastrous consequences, as we shall shortly see.

To sum up. Chastity and maternity were held in high regard in Rome, as ideals that is, and for purely practical purposes. The Vestal Virgins, six of them, who tended the undying fire on the very hearth of Rome, the ladies with whom noble Romans deposited their wills, who had special seats of honour allotted to them in the theatre, these were the true models of Roman purity. The Great Mother, the first foreign goddess to be imported into Rome, during the second Punic War, was greeted by the noblest matrons of Rome. These included an ancestress of the first empress, who, when the raft carrying the image went aground, vowed that she could haul it clear with her girdle, as proof of her chastity, which she triumphantly did. Thus early we see this double eulogy of maternity and chastity, which shone all the more brightly against the shocking background of male unchastity, itself aggravated by the promiscuity which slavery always promotes.

When it came to adultery and divorce, there was one law for the women and none for the men. Augustus, it is true, did try to amend the lax morals of his time—for others, that is. A law was passed to encourage married fecundity, in place of footloose bachelorhood. As Dio tartly comments, the fact that it was sponsored by two bachelors "shewed how necessary it was". Augustus also tightened up, on paper and in women's favour, the law relating to adultery. But when he himself was so notoriously enterprising, and both his daughter and granddaughter were bywords for lechery, it was not to be supposed that his legislation would have much effect where effect was most needed, that is in court circles.

The situation is given a balanced exposition by Hugh Last in Volume X of the *Cambridge Ancient History*:

The high conception of the relation between husband and wife in early Rome is scarcely more remarkable than the lack of legal regulations to protect it. All unions except the negligible minority contracted by the elaborate process of *confarreatio* [a primitive but binding ceremony into which entered as the name implies cakes of barley-meal of which our modern wedding-cake is the vestigial analogue] might be dissolved without the intervention of the state, and in marriage even the formalities which brought the wife under the *manus* of her husband ceased to be necessary before the time of the Twelve Tables [450 BC]. Not only did women remain in the *potestas* of the *paterfamilias*, but in course of time arrangements were devised whereby her dowry ceased to pass irrecoverably to her husband. . . . The change in the status of the dowry marks a change in the position of women themselves. Though they had enjoyed an honourable prominence in daily life from the earliest times of which records are preserved, there are elements in Roman law which clearly assume a high degree of subjection to the husband: the most famous of all is the denial of the remedy for adultery by the husband, though adultery on the other side was an act for which the husband might even put his wife to death. But, by the last century of the Republic, females had in practice obtained their independence, and nothing but social convention and a sense of responsibility barred the way to a dangerous exploitation of their privilege.

The result was inevitable. There were of course decent couples in all walks of life, specially among the provincials and peasantry, faithful and loyal, true helpmates and good parents. The poet Horace proclaims it and the surly Tacitus admits it. Even in Rome, it was a single class which was chiefly infected by the new frivolity; but that class, the governing nobility, it was essential to preserve. Hence Augustus' legislation.

It might be supposed that this ambivalent position of women, in particular of the nobility, would be ameliorated when it became legally possible for a woman to share the life of Rome's supreme ruler, that is by becoming Caesar's wife. On the contrary, it greatly increased her peril, both physical and moral. It was one thing to be a matron, even an intriguing or bossy matron, quite another to be a ruler or a ruler's consort. The most famous matron of them all, Cornelia, daughter of Scipio Africanus, had been given in marriage to Tiberius Sempronius Gracchus. When he died, the reigning Ptolemy, king of Egypt, wanted to make her his consort. Cornelia held it to be a nobler destiny to be 'the mother of the Gracchi' than to be a foreign queen. In Roman eyes it was. Queens were not highly regarded in Rome. Semiramis of Babylon had been a vicious tyrant. Another queen, perhaps equally draped in legend, was Dido of Carthage. Virgil extols his hero Aeneas for deserting her, because he put Rome first—an attitude which every Roman applauded. Most outstanding of all was Cleopatra, the crocodile queen who had bewitched first Julius Caesar and then Antony, the only one of Rome's enemies since Hannibal, and a woman at that, who had struck fear into the heart of Rome.

Was Rome now to admit a queen, an empress, to the Palatine, to the very hearth of Romulus, from which kings had been expelled all those centuries ago? Rome was to do exactly that. But what a burden it would be for the women thus dangerously exalted. To add to all their other disabilities, this eminence was to be their ultimate abasement, the dizzy pinnacle from which so many would be hurled headlong. Fortunately for Rome, and for Rome's posterity, the very first Roman lady to become the First Lady of Rome had a head for heights. Her name was Livia, and she was the wife of Augustus.

Part I

CHAPTER I

Livia Augusta

Who can adequately express his astonishment at the changes of fortune and the mysterious ups and downs of human affairs? Who must not either hope for a change for the better, or fear one for the worse? Look at Livia. The daughter of Drusus Claudianus, a man of the highest distinction and courage, and herself the most eminent of Roman ladies by reason of her birth, integrity and beauty, Livia, whom we were later to see as the wife of Augustus, and after his translation to the gods, his priestess and his daughter [by adoption in Augustus' will], here she was fleeing from the troops of the very Caesar who was soon to be her husband, carrying at her breast an infant scarcely two years old, our present emperor Tiberius, the upholder of the Roman empire and destined to be the son of this same Caesar [by legal adoption].

She made her way by unfrequented tracks, to escape the swords of the soldiers, with only one attendant to avoid recognition, She reached the sea, and with her husband Nero sailed off to Sicily.

THUS DOES VELLEIUS PATERCULUS, writing in AD 30, give us in his *Roman History Primer* this vivid epitome of the great empress who had died the year before. Hers is indeed one of the great true-life Cinderella stories of all time. But first of all, who was Livia?

Livia herself was by blood really a Claudia. She was a scion of the great Claudian house, which had given so many eminent men to Rome, among them Appius Claudius, the blind censor who was consul in 307 BC and again in 296, the first clear-cut personality in Roman history—for thus early had this family the genius for eminence. To him Rome owed its first aqueduct, and its first great road, the Queen of Roads, which is still called after him the Via Appia. A later Appius Claudius commanded the first Roman army to operate outside Italy, at the invasion of Sicily in 264 BC. Tiberius Gracchus, the tribune and social reformer of the mid-second century BC, married a Claudia, daughter of yet another representative of this famous family who was *princeps senatus*, Leader of the House, as we might say, though the parallel is not exact.

It is important to remember Livia's Claudian heritage, not only because it contributed so notably to her prestige, but also for a sadder and more sinister reason. There was in the Claudians a deep-seated, ingrained streak of madness, which was to manifest itself in more than one of the imperial progeny. Livia's father had been adopted into yet another of Rome's first families, the Livii Drusi. That is why she was called Livia and not Claudia.

It was of this doubly splendid Livian-Claudian lineage that the future empress was born on the 30th January in 57 BC. Marcus Livius Drusus had been tribune in 91, and was assassinated by an enemy who resented his efforts to appease Rome's Italian allies and to bring about political and social harmony. His life, as Mommsen puts it, really was conducted in the belief that *noblesse oblige*. This man's son, Livia's father, Marcus Livius Drusus II, was an ardent republican. He was proscribed in 42 after Philippi by the triumvirs (one of whom was the future Augustus himself) and committed suicide. Livia was already married to a distant relative—fifteen was by no means too young for matrimony in an epoch which held that old age started at forty—Tiberius Claudius Nero. He too was a good republic-man, and was one of those who voted that the assassins who struck down Julius Caesar in 44 should be publicly rewarded. In 40 BC he was in charge of a garrison in Campania. He tried to organise a slave revolt, which was soon crushed. Octavian, who was only twenty-three, realised that all opposition to him was now at an end, and that clemency was the best policy. He therefore suffered Tiberius Claudius Nero, his wife Livia, and their infant son Tiberius, to flee to Sicily, thus by what Dio calls one of the strangest paradoxes of history (as indeed it was), allowing his future empress and his successor as

emperor to avoid retribution. The sad little trio moved on to
Greece, where they had a narrow escape. They were caught in
a forest fire and Livia's clothing, even her hair, were singed. The
people of Sparta treated them so kindly that nineteen years later,
Augustus, finding himself in Greece, attended the Spartans'
public messes (banquets they could not be called) and gave them
the island of Cythera, which lies off the south-east promontory
of the Peloponnese. The family were not exiles for long, because
after the so-called treaty of Brundisium between Octavian and
Antony in October of that same year 40, they returned to Italy
where they lived in grateful obscurity. By the treaty of Misenum
between the two rivals and Sextus son of Pompey in 39, Livia's
husband was reinstated. The sequel strikes us as disgusting;
but as already said, the nearer we get to the Romans the harder
it is to understand them. What followed was a typically Roman
transaction. In any discussion of Roman affairs, political or personal, we must rid our minds at the very outset of any modern
ideas of loyalty. There were loyal Romans of both sexes, and we
shall meet several of them; but loyalty as such is a sense of
obligation arising from the chivalrous view of life. Chivalry
was unknown to the Romans, just as it was unknown to the
French revolutionaries. Talleyrand or Fouché, each betraying
his emperor in his own way, would have been quite at home in
imperial Rome. Tiberius Claudius Nero had commanded Julius
Caesar's fleet during the Alexandrine war of 47 BC. He had
helped to establish colonies in southern Gaul. He was praetor in
42 (or 41). In the so-called Perusine war of 41, Tiberius was on
the side of Antony's brother, that is Caesar's enemy, and as we
have seen started an abortive revolt in Campania. Now Caesar's
'son' and heir Octavian was lord of the ascendant, and so to him
Tiberius must be as pliant as a reed, as ready to give as Caesar
was to receive. If Caesar wanted his wife, Caesar must have her.
That Livia was pregnant with his second child need be no obstacle. Octavian was already married to Scribonia, to whom he
had been joined in political wedlock a year before, as her third
husband, Octavian, who though twice betrothed had never
actually tasted the bitter waters of matrimony, found Scribonia
unbearable: she was a shrew. And here was Livia—still only
eighteen years old. He was determined to have her.

On the very day that Scribonia gave birth to their daughter
Julia, Octavian divorced her, this 'political animal' as a modern

scholar has described woman in the eyes of Octavian. This rejection was to bring untold unhappiness to both daughter and father. To obtain Livia, Octavian induced the pontiffs to declare that even if a wife were pregnant, as Livia was, it was legitimate for her to be divorced and to remarry. Her complacent husband Tiberius gave her away as though he were her father, and the wedding was duly solemnised, just three months before Livia gave birth to her second (and last) child, Nero Claudius Drusus. Octavian, as the future Augustus was still known, 'acknowledged' the child—a formality which ensured his legitimacy—and then sent him back to his real father, making a note in his memorandum-book: 'Caesar'—as he legally called himself by virtue of his adoption—"Caesar returned to his father Nero the child born by Livia his wife." This was in 38 BC. Poor Nero lived for another five years and left Octavian as guardian of both his children by Livia, Tiberius and Drusus. The gossips had had a grand time. "Lucky people can have a baby in three months," they said. Nor could they fail to dine out on the story that at the wedding-party a little boy, such as great Roman houses used to keep to run about and prattle, generally naked, the human originals of the Renaissance *putti*, seeing Livia and Octavian on one couch, and Nero on another, asked Livia: "What are you doing here, mistress? your husband's over there?"

Thus did Augustus—it is simpler to give him the name he was so soon to acquire, the name he bequeathed to an age—embark with Livia on half a century of devotion and glory. What kind of beings were these two?

Of Augustus, Suetonius, his first biographer, (because alas Plutarch never wrote the life he intended to write) has this to say. We must listen to Philemon Holland, the 'translator in ordinary' of the Elizabethan and Jacobean ages:

He was of an excellent presence and personage, and the same throughout all degrees of his age most lovely and amiable, negligible though he were of all manner of pikedness [elegance], for combing and trimming of his head so careless, as that he would use at once many barbers, such as came to hand, it skilled not whom; and onewhile he clipped and anotherwhile he shaved his beard, and yet at the very same time he either read or wrote somewhat. His visage and countenance, whether he spake or held his peace, was so mild, so pleasant and lightsome,

Empress Livia, the wife of Augustus, from a statue in the National
Museum, Naples

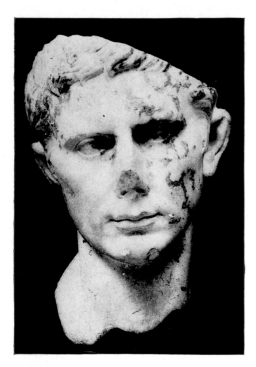

a) Augustus

b) Livia

c) The deified Augustus. A coin struck in the principate of Caligula, AD 37–41

d) The development of the Roman male countenance from the almost Simian features of Republican man to the handsome if sometimes coarse or brutal faces of the Empire is as marked and inexplicable as the facial difference between the Englishman of the age of Elizabeth I and that of Victoria. (From a tomb relief, first century BC.)

that one of the nobles and potentates of Gaul confessed unto his countrymen, he was thereby only restrained and reclaimed that he did not approach near unto him under colour of conference, as he passed over the Alps, and so shove him down a steep crag to break his neck, as his full intent was. He had a pair of clear and shining eyes, wherein also (as he would have men believe) was seated a kind of divine vigour; and he joyed much if a man looking wistly upon him held down his face, as it were against the brightness of the sun. But in old age he saw not very well with the left eye. His teeth grew thin in his head, and the same were small and ragged: the hair of his head was somewhat curled and turning downward, and withal of a light-yellow colour. His eyebrows met together; his ears were of a mean bigness; his nose both in the upper part bearing out round, and also beneath somewhat the longest. Of colour and complexion he was between a brown and fair white. His stature was short; and yet Julius Marathus his freedman writeth in the history of his life that he was five feet and nine inches [5 feet 7 inches by English measure]. But as low as the same was, the proportionable making and feature of his limbs hid it so as it might not be perceived, unless he were compared with some taller person standing by. His left thigh was weak, so that he sometimes limped. He was very sensitive to cold, so much so that his right hand would become numb, and unable to hold a pen, even when fitted with a horn finger-stall. His digestion was not good. He suffered from gravel. He found travel tiresome, always preferring the sea to the land. Even to reach Tivoli or Palestrina he would take two days.

This description of the great ruler is clearly authentic. Suetonius was at one time a court official, had access to official records, and would have known men and women whose parents remembered Augustus. What is of interest to us is this: as a young man, Augustus was not all that handsome: the coin now in the British Museum struck at Ephesus when he was twenty-two shows a hard-faced little schemer. Compare it with the later portraits, such as the Meroë bronze, also in the British Museum, or the Boston head, or the Vatican statue. Idealised? Yes, but the cardinal fact is that he *was* idealised. Tacitus says that the only emperor up to his age who improved with age instead of deteriorating was Vespasian. He should have included Augustus. He improved all the time.

Unfortunately we have no such literary close-up of Livia as we have of Augustus. That she was beautiful and chaste her contemporary Velleius has already told us. She was also, as we learn from other sources, a woman of ambition, and of a dominating disposition, another trait which she inherited on both sides from the Claudians: it came out particularly in their women. Livia's statues show a calm, determined matron of noble tranquillity in mien and stance. In fact Livia reminds us strikingly of the early Victorian portraits by Beechey, with the same simplicity, even the same style of hair-dressing. Fortunately, with Livia, we can get a rather more stereoscopic view, not from what she looked like, but from what she liked looking at. Preserved in Rome are chambers from two of her houses. The first, and simpler, is still in what is called Livia's house on the Palatine, the home of Augustus it was really, but that it should be known as Livia's is significant. The man who slept on the same low bed for forty years was not going to be a connoisseur of interior decoration. The house is small: only later did the vast erections which made the Palatine the original of our word palace come into being; but it is very attractive. The walls are painted in a *trompe l'œil* architectural style reminiscent of Pompeii, with which indeed it was contemporary. They are charming, these rooms, and very feminine, Livia's choice beyond question, for in Livia's own villa at Prima Porta, north of Rome, there stood one of the most exquisite chambers ever created, now preserved for us in the *Terme* museum in Rome. It must originally have been designed as an underground, or at least a windowless room, such as the Romans were fond of using as a refuge against the heat—the *sirdab* of modern Iraq. On Hadrian's villa below Tivoli we even find the ultra-modern device of a water-cooled roof.

What is so striking about this room from Livia's villa is the 'green felicity' of its decoration, in utter contrast with the 'architectural' style, framing mythological scenes, in general vogue (though there is in the Fitzwilliam Museum at Cambridge a mosaic niche of similar naturalistic style from Baiae). It is, in the words of the late Eugénie Strong,

a masterpiece of Roman illusionism—the garden enclosure painted on the walls of a room in the villa of the Empress

Livia at Prima Porta. The conquest of 'space beyond' is here an accomplished fact—the sense of the confining wall is annulled; it is as if the closed door, beyond which in certain Pompeian paintings we see trees waving and birds flitting, had suddenly burst open and we had entered an enchanted garden. It is an *hortus inclusus* of purest delight, where the flowers bloom, the birds sing and the butterflies flutter, without the intrusion of any human element. In the Prima Porta fresco it is no longer the wall that encloses the room, but the garden itself that defines the space by means of a well-trimmed path running between two railings, the innermost of which breaks now and then into exedrae adorned by tall conifers.

Thus does one talented and perceptive woman describe the setting of another. A second reminder of Livia from Prima Porta, and a poignant one at that, is the marble head of a little prince, now in the Museo Barraco in Rome. There he is, this alert and determined little man, a true Claudian—if he ever survived to be one. Beloved he clearly was: perhaps he died young.

Why was Livia so called? The answer to this question is as simple as it is sad. Some of the disabilities of Roman women were mentioned in the Introduction. We now have to record one more—the grudging way in which they were named. Under the Republic they had no personal names at all. Roman male nomenclature was perfectly simple. Every Roman had two names, every 'respectable' Roman three, a forename, a family name and a distinguishing or nickname. To take two of the best known Romans as examples, Marcus Tullius Cicero and Gaius Julius Caesar. Marcus and Gaius were personal forenames, like Thomas or Richard, Tullius and Julius were family names, like Jones or Smith. Cicero and Caesar were nicknames, given to some ancestor, and so borne by their descendants. 'Cicero' is plain: it means a chickpea, and was given to one of Marcus' ancestors who had a nick in the end of his nose which resembled that vegetable (*Cicer arietinum*). Just what Caesar meant cannot be determined. Was it that (as many ancient authorities thought) a former Julius has been cut (*cæsus*) from his mother's womb? (Julius Caesar was, by an operation which in his honour we still call 'Caesarian'). Or was it that he had a fine crop of hair (*caesaries*), or had grey-blue eyes (*caeruleus*) or even had killed an elephant 'which in Africa they call Caesar'? Such is the disputed origin of a name which was to become the most exalted title ever known, and lasted into our own day as Tsar and Kaiser.

No such individuality was permitted to women. They were known simply by the feminine form of the family *nomen*, which became a sort of family laundry-mark or luggage label. Julius Caesar had an aunt who was called Julia. He had two sisters, each also called Julia. So was his daughter by Cornelia. That makes four. Augustus' daughter (he having been adopted into the Julian house) was called Julia; so was his granddaughter. So by testamentary adoption was Livia herself. So were Tiberius' granddaughters—nine Julias in the imperial family in little over a century. Dr Balsdon* informs us that:

> Under the Empire, this strict economy in women's names broke down. Two names for a woman were common, the first her family name, the second taken from her father's third name or even from her mother; and it was often this second name which was commonly used. As a result, in many cases one confusion replaced another. For the wife of Germanicus [really Vipsania Agrippina] and her daughter, the mother of Nero [whose name was Julia Agrippina] were both known as Agrippina.

The apotheosis of childhood in sculpture is to be found in the *Ara Pacis*, the altar of peace, now once again reassembled and worthily housed on the bank of the Tiber next to Augustus' mausoleum. Here the children are individual beings, charming, wayward little creatures, living their own lives, as children do, unperturbed by the goings-on of the grand grown-ups with whom they associate or disassociate, as the whim takes them. It is by no means far-fetched to see in this marble multitude the caressing hand of the empress who, being herself beautiful, attracted and loved beauty. Indeed, the figure of the Mother (Earth or Italy) on the enclosure wall of the altar may well have been taken from Livia herself: this is no mythological evocation, it is a living, breathing woman. A comparison of this relief with the statue of Livia in the Naples museum makes the identification more than probable. After noting the prominence given to the imperial children in this great monument, which was assembled between 13 and 9 BC, Dr Eugénie Strong makes the significant comment: "It is not so much with the majesty of Empire that the *Ara Pacis*

* Balsdon, J. P. V. D., *Roman Women*, Bodley Head.

strikes one as with the human and personal conception of the Principate which Augustus wished to stress." Whence had Augustus acquired this conception? There can be only one source: the dates inexorably exclude any other.

Agrippa, Augustus' exact coeval, and one of the greatest prime ministers of all time, had died in 12 BC. Maecenas, a lesser but still brilliant light, in 8. Only Livia was left now. For twenty-two more years she was to be his guide, counsellor and sole comforter. But she was far more than that: she had a radical influence on her husband's character. As so often in contemplating Augustus and Livia, we seem to see Victoria and Albert in reverse. Not that Victoria was ever as hard-natured as the young Octavian; but the transformation of the wayward princess into the august sovereign was as remarkable as the metamorphosis of the triumvir into the Father of his Country; and in each case the influence of the consort was paramount. Even in antiquity it was remarked that Augustus seemed to have been transformed from brutality to benignity. Writing in the fourth century, Julian the Apostate, son of Constantine the Great, in his little squib entitled *The Caesars*, attributes the metamorphosis to the Stoic principles which Augustus imbibed from his tutor Athenodorus of Tarsus, and from the writings of Posidonius, a philosopher much admired during the first half of the last century BC. But this influence was fleeting, nor did it prevent the young Octavian from committing atrociously cruel acts. He took only too active a part at the age of twenty in the proscriptions of 200 senators and 2,000 knights, including Cicero himself, which followed on the victory of Philippi. During this same triumvirate he is recorded to have ordered a knight called Pinarius, who was taking notes of a speech young Caesar was making to the troops, to be stabbed then and there as a spy. A praetor called Quintus Gallius held some folded writing-tablets under his cloak as he was paying his respects. Octavian, thinking he was concealing a sword had him hustled out of the assembly and tortured. When he made no confession, Caesar ordered his execution, first tearing out his eyes with his own hands. Later on he had the legs of his secretary broken for taking a bribe; and when the tutor and attendants of his grandson Caius behaved arrogantly he had them thrown into the Tiber with weights round their necks.

Gradually, Livia tamed the brute in the man; or perhaps, with her woman's instinct, realised that (as Plato had pictured

it in his beautiful allegory) there are in every man the two steeds,
the unruly and the noble, and set herself to nurture the noble.
This seems all the more likely, in that Octavian's own sister
Octavia was a woman of truly saintly character.

There were aspects of her husband's character which not even
Livia could change. To us, his pathological superstition seems
laughable; but to Livia it would not have so appeared. She was
superstitious herself. The site of her villa at Prima Porta was
decided by the fact that shortly after her marriage to the future
emperor, an eagle threw a white hen, with a sprig of laurel in
its mouth, into Livia's lap as she sat there. Livia cared for the bird,
and planted the laurel, which took root and provided the wreaths
for those who celebrated triumphs. She humoured her husband,
therefore, when he wore a seal-skin as a talisman against thunder;
and when an electric storm broke over Rome, he its lord and
master, retired to an underground chamber in the belief that
lightning would only penetrate five feet deep. "And Livia was
destined to hold in her lap even Caesar's power (as she had held
that hen) and to dominate him in everything." Or nearly everything: just occasionally he could refuse her requests, as when she
sought Roman citizenship for a Gaulish protégé. Augustus was
very touchy on this subject. He refused the citizenship, but
granted the Gaul immunity from taxation instead.

Moderation was what Livia desired. She preferred to banish
the dreadful memories of the civil wars, and of the years before
she met Augustus. When her grandson Claudius, the future
emperor who had literary leanings, proposed to write the history
of those evil times, Livia restrained him from doing so. In the
year AD 4, thirty years that is after Augustus had become formally
and *de jure* master of Rome, a certain Gnaeus Cornelius formed a
plot against him. Augustus naturally enough was much perturbed,
and puzzled as to what he should do. Just as the Prince Consort
committed his thoughts to paper before discussing any important
topic with Queen Victoria, so did Augustus before seeking
Livia's advice. On this occasion Dio gives us a long résumé of
what they said to each other. This is, of course, a literary arti-
fice; but Dio would not have inserted it unless it really did
reflect Augustus' dependence on his wife's counsel. Was he to
punish Cornelius? That would breed enmity, but it might deter
others. Livia was ready with a typically sensible plan. "Where
one man rules," she said, "plots are inevitable, often hatched

by the ruler's so-called 'friends'." It was an occupational hazard.
If the ruler proceeded against one, he would stir up endless
strife, nor would he ever be safe. No, the right course was to
pardon Cornelius, nay more, treat him with generosity. As
usual, Augustus took Livia's advice. He even advanced Cornelius
to the consulate. Livia had saved his life. Who would now be
more grateful to the imperial couple? There were no more plots.

Augustus rewarded Livia with every dignity it was in his
power to bestow. She was, like Augustus' sister Octavia, granted
the tribunician sacrosanctity. She was honoured with statues,
and not only in Rome. We can still read, for instance, the inscription on the base of one such erected in the fashionable spa of
Epidaurus in the Peloponnese. She was granted the privileges
attaching to a parent of three children, for Augustus' legislation
laid down that parents who had produced their quota might
henceforth accept legacies without restriction. The father,
among other benefits, received accelerated promotion if he was in
public life. The mother if not already independent in law,
acquired full legal independence. In Livia's case, as often in later
reigns, the award was honorary, because she had two children
only, her sons Tiberius and Drusus by her first husband. Her
union with Augustus produced no joint heir. She conceived
once, but miscarried. She had in any case been freed from the
patria potestas in 35 BC. Legal independence meant much to
Livia, because she was a very rich woman. Besides estates in
many parts of Italy, she owned property in Asia Minor, Gaul
and Palestine. Herod the Great was a personal friend of Augustus,
and Livia formed a by no means creditable, but very lucrative,
alliance with Herod's sister. She reaped a rich reward. Livia
also owned mines in Spain, which, in Buchan's words in her
day, "was to Rome what Peru was to Spain herself in the sixteenth century, an almost fabulous Eldorado". She had a personal
staff of over 1000.

So long as Augustus lived, Livia kept, or perhaps was kept,
modestly in the background. When a fire broke out down in the
Forum, just below her own home on the Palatine, Livia was
rebuked for going to help the fire-fighters: that was no part of an
empress's duties; it put her too prominently, too personally, in
the public eye, however beneficient her presence might have been.
(She probably got in the way.) When a state banquet was to be
given in honour of Drusus, Augustus entertained the male

guests on the Capitol: Livia had to hold a separate reception for the ladies.

None of the poets who lavish praise on Augustus mentions his wife. In the palace itself she would spin and weave her husband's garments. When his eyes roved, as they so often did, she kept hers modestly averted. It was even said that she had assisted Augustus in his extra-marital exploration. Augustus once made her enter a beauty-contest with Terentia, the wife of Maecenas, for whom he was known to have a liking. Livia herself was, physically speaking, above suspicion. One day, she met a band of naked men—presumably on the beach, or coming from the gymnasium. They were at once destined for death. Livia saved them by saying that to a chaste woman naked men were no more than statues.

In AD 14 Augustus died. For more than half a century Livia had been at his side, his constant comforter and counsellor, ever present to encourage or to restrain. He died in her arms, murmuring: "Farewell Livia; live mindful of our marriage."

The great Augustan age, the age which this great woman had done so much to create and to maintain was over. Rome would not look upon her like again.

CHAPTER II

Damnosa Hereditas—The Julio-Claudian Curse

EVER SINCE THE year 1837, the widow of an English monarch has been regarded with respectful veneration deepening in the twentieth century into admiration and affection, haloed indeed with an aura of devotion such as is bestowed in Catholic countries on the more potent and popular saints. An English reader would therefore naturally suppose that Livia, the woman who for fifty-two years had been the spouse of Rome's master and regenerator, would be similarly regarded. She was not; on the contrary she was traduced, mistrusted and accused of every sort of intrigue, even of murder. How did this reversal of her former felicity come about?

The answer is that it was largely due to her own conduct, and to that of her late husband. Above all, to their family. The irony of the situation lies in the very fact that they two themselves had no family, no child of their own. Had they been the parents of a son, even of a daughter, the whole destiny of the *imperium*, the empire, would have been different, and far happier. As it was, it was their very childlessness that produced what a jurist of the next century was to describe in the famous phrase *damnosa hereditas*, ruinous inheritance.

The family tree of the Julio-Claudian clan is dauntingly obscured by undergrowth and suckers. Let us therefore just outline the main branches, as they affect Livia and her successors, thus:

1. Livia and Augustus—barren union.
2. Livia by her former husband, two sons, Tiberius and Drusus.
3. Augustus by his former wife, one daughter, Julia.

That looks simple enough, and there appears no reason why the family fabric should decay as it did. At first all went well. Livia behaved just as a royal widow should behave. She escorted her husband's corpse from Nola, where he had died, to the mausoleum, the Augustan Frogmore, which still stands there by the Tiber, and mourned by the funeral pyre for five days. She then with her own hands placed the ashes in the burial-chamber. She left the palace and retired to one of her own dwelling-places.

Livia had always been frank about her hold upon Augustus. Too frank, in fact. Someone once asked her how she had won her ascendancy over him. Instead of deprecating the enquiry, Livia answered that it was by being scrupulously chaste herself, doing gladly whatever he wanted, and never meddling in his affairs; in particular pretending not to hear, not even to notice the favourites, male and female, who were the objects of his passion. This declaration, even had it been true (and it was at best a half-truth), was to say the least of it priggish, just as the ostentatious simplicity of her home-industries was priggish.

That Livia was very rich has already been noted. By Augustus' will, she became far richer. She inherited a third of his estate, an exceptional grant, far greater than a less privileged widow might hope for, which by law was a mere 100,000 sesterces. By this same will she was adopted into the Julian clan. She was proclaimed Julia Augusta. She gave a cool million to the senator Numerius, who swore that he had seen Augustus ascending to heaven like Romulus. She then became the priestess of the cult of her deified husband, and was allowed a lictor to go before her when acting as such. Trifles? Yes, but irritating trifles. Rich women are seldom loved. Intriguing women even less. Livia was both. Her relations with the fascinating if raffish family of the Herods has already been mentioned. When Herod the Great built his new city in Samaria and called it, after the emperor, Sebaste, that is in Greek Augusta, the empress lavished the most costly furnishings upon it. As we know, she reaped a rich reward, but the transaction, bartering with Levantine princes, did not please old-fashioned Romans.

All this might have been forgiven to such a venerable figure as Livia but for the fierce light which beat upon her by reason of the misbehaviour of Augustus' daughter and granddaughter. But what is sad is that, all in all, the posthumous image of the great Livia, Rome's greatest empress, should have become so besmirched, and should have remained so. Contemporaries praised her—Velleius' encomium has already been mentioned. When she died he called her "a woman pre-eminent among women, and who in all things resembled the gods more than mankind, whose power no one felt except for the alleviation of danger or the promotion of dignity". She had the beauty of Venus, the character of Juno, said the poet Ovid, nostalgically recalling her from his Black Sea exile.

The mud stuck, as mud usually does. Dio, writing nearly 200 years later, can say this: "It was said that Tiberius had secured the empire through Livia, contrary to the will of Augustus." This was quite untrue, but the introduction of Tiberius in this context is of great significance. Tiberius made it clear that he had been given it by the Senate, not by Livia, whom he detested. But see how the calumny persisted. In the same chapter (Book LVI, 14) Dio continues:

Tiberius bade Livia to conduct herself in a 'democratic' fashion, so far as it was permissible for her to do so, partly in order to imitate him, partly to prevent her from being over-proud. For she occupied a very exalted position, far above all women of former days. Whenever she wanted to, she could receive the Senate, and such of the people who wished to attend her 'drawing-rooms', and their names were duly published in the Court Circular. For a time, letters of Tiberius bore her signature, and communications were addressed to both alike. Except that she never ventured to enter the senate-chamber or the camps, she undertook to manage everything as if she were sole ruler. For in the time of Augustus she possessed the greatest influence and she always declared it was she who had made Tiberius emperor. Consequently, she was not content to rule on equal terms with him, but wished to take precedence over him. As a result many extraordinary measures were proposed; some people said she should be styled Mother of the Country, others Parent. Yet others proposed that Tiberius be named after her, meaning that as Greeks were named for their fathers, he should be called after his mother. Tiberius was much annoyed, and would not sanction the proposed honours to be voted for her, with a few exceptions, nor allow her any extravagances of conduct. For instance she had once dedicated in her house an image of

Augustus and in honour of the event wanted to banquet the
Senate and the knights, with their wives. Tiberius vetoed the
whole affair until the Senate had agreed to it, and then only
allowed her to receive the women. Then he removed her
entirely from public affairs, but allowed her to direct matters at
home. Finally, as she was tiresome even there, he kept away
from Rome and avoided her as much as he could. It was on
her account that he went to Capri. Livia died at the age of
eighty-six. Tiberius neither visited her during her illness,
nor laid out her body. He paid her no honour, and absolutely
forbade her 'deification'. The Senate ordered a year's mourning
for Livia, and voted her an arch—an honour conferred on
no other woman, because she had saved the lives of not a few
of them, had brought up the children of many of them, and
helped to pay their daughters' dowries. She was hailed by some
as the Mother of her Country. She was buried in the mausoleum. Tiberius paid none of her bequests.

(It was only Tiberius' successor, Gaius Caligula, who executed
her will.)

An analysis of this obituary by Dio is of great interest. All
the old calumnies are raked up. That Livia was proud, even to the
point of being over-bearing, cannot be denied. That was her
Claudian heritage, reinforced by sixty years of unprecedented
dominance. But what remains with us is the impression of a great
and good woman, a woman with a few failings, rather obvious
and obtrusive failings, but predominantly good, generous and
virtuous. What is equally clear is that her son Tiberius was a
boor.

Even good parents can breed bad sons, making them a sort
of sump, as it were, for the impurities so happily drained away
from their own pure personalities. That is what had happened to
Tiberius.

He was not Cæsar's son. Nor had he been allowed to be his
father's son. When he was an infant of only four, he was to see
his mother snatched away by the very man who had caused his
parents to become refugees and outcasts. As a child, therefore,
he had a double reason for disliking his stepfather. As he grew
older, the mutual dislike between Augustus and Tiberius
deepened. It was accentuated by two domestic disasters. Young
Tiberius really did prefigure Tennyson's 'divinely gifted man'.

Who breaks his birth's invidious bar
And grasps the skirts of happy chance
And breasts the blows of circumstance,
And grapples with his evil star.

Tiberius, be it remembered, was a Claudian on both sides, with Claudian pride, and Claudian ability. As a young man of twenty-two, he accompanied Augustus to the Levant, and received back from the Parthian king the standards and the surviving prisoners who had been lost in the appalling disaster of 53 BC. Rome went wild with joy. Augustus at the close of his life records the diplomatic victory in his *Res Gestae*. Tiberius brought back the trophies, but Augustus took the credit. He already knew Tiberius well. As a boy of twelve he had ridden beside Augustus during his triumph. Two years later he was with the emperor in Spain. On both occasions his companion was his exact coeval Marcellus, son of Augustus' sister Octavia. Clearly, both were in the running for the succession. Which was it to be? In 25 Caesar made his decision: the nephew won, and the stepson lost. Marcellus married Julia, Caesar's only child, his daughter by his former wife Scribonia. Tiberius now realised that the supreme station was not for him. With admirable, Claudian, resolution he opted for a military career. From the year 20 BC until AD 12, with only an interval to be mentioned shortly, he showed himself to be a brilliant general. In AD 12 he returned to Rome after restoring the situation in Germany, created by a humiliation comparable to that of Carrhae, the slaughter of Varus and his three legions. He had besides married a woman to whom he was devoted, Vipsania Agrippina, daughter of the great Vipsanius Agrippa, and granddaughter of Cicero's confidant Atticus.

But already, in 12 BC, his sun was occluded. Marcellus, the prince charming, had died after only two years of marriage, that is in 23. Julia, the princess royal, was once again on the market. Augustus gave her to Agrippa in the year 21. (After the death of Vipsania's mother, he was now married to Marcellus' sister, that is to a niece of Augustus, but she was easily disposed of.) Thus in the year 20 BC, Tiberius on marrying Vipsania found himself son-in-law of the princess royal. Cramping, no doubt of it, but worse, far worse, was to come. In 12 BC, Agrippa himself died, after begetting a daughter and three sons. So Caesar now had an assured succession, or so it seemed, and Tiberius could pursue his promising career, loving and loved by Vipsania, and their little boy, now perhaps in his second year.

Then the imperial thunderbolt struck. Tiberius must marry Julia. Yes, by imperial command, he was to marry his mother-in-law. Vipsania was never to be an empress. Tiberius saw her only once again. He broke down and cried. He was never allowed to see her a second time. Vipsania lived on for another thirty-two years. She married again, a senator called Gaius Asinius Gallus, a prominent politician who caused much embarrassment to Tiberius, to whom he fell a victim three years after Vipsania's death. Although she was never to enter the palace as its mistress, she had the satisfaction of seeing her soldier son Drusus hailed in public triumph just before she died. "Of Agrippa's children she alone died peacefully", is the ominous epitaph of Tacitus. Tiberius' marriage to Julia was disastrous, as it was bound to be. He had to watch her two elder sons by her marriage to Agrippa grow up to be Caesar's preferred favourites, cherished grandsons who were clearly destined for the purple. The third son was a crazy lout, who was banished to an island. The daughter, Agrippina, married into the reigning house. Tiberius and Julia had one son, who died in infancy. Tiberius can hardly have wanted more: he was so obviously now a second-class prince. He kept out of Rome as much as he could, campaigning in the north. Finally, in exasperation, in the year 6 BC, he retired to Rhodes. To cover the breakdown in the family fabric which this advertised, he was granted a sort of high commissionership. But no one was deceived. While he was in Rhodes, Augustus sent him a bill of divorcement: he was no longer the husband even of Julia. Nor would Julia ever be the wife of a Caesar.

With Tiberius, who must have seen in his stepfather ruthlessness and hostility, condoned by what he could only regard as his mother's callous preference for power before maternal obligation—with this doubly outcast prince we can but sympathise. His whole character was warped by the inhuman way he had been treated; and by the age of forty he was psychologically ruined. As he had been given, so he was to give, which largely accounts for the sombre picture Tacitus has painted of him. He never forgave his mother.

But Julia too engages our sympathy. What a picturesque empress she would have made. Her mother Scribonia had twice been married before young Octavian took her on, and divorced her the next year. It must have been from her that Julia inherited her witty, skittish temperament. In any case, how could she have respected, far less loved, her father who had sloughed off her mother on the very day on which Julia was born? still less could she have been on any terms of affection with Livia, who had supplanted her mother. At the age of fourteen this sprightly princess royal was married to Marcellus. As suggested above, this meant that she had every prospect of becoming empress. No longer would she be constrained by Livia to engage in the cottage industries on the Palatine, no longer would her cold father be able to forbid her consorting with amusing males: he had actually sent a curt note to one of them, telling him not to be so presumptuous as to call on his daughter when she was staying in the royal pavilion at Baiae. No longer was she to be rebuked for being the centre of attraction for the younger set at the gladiatorial games, while Livia received the *vieillesse dorée*. It may surprise us to find either of these ladies at such bestial exhibitions, but females did attend them, and even fought in them.

Here is a description of what Julia must have experienced as she sat there in the circus with her young friends:

Nor was this fascination surprising, for no pageant has ever combined more powerful elements of attraction. The magnificent circus [not of course for Julia the Colosseum, which was not built until AD 79], the gorgeous dresses of the assembled Court, the contagion of a passionate enthusiasm thrilling almost visibly through the mighty throng, the breathless silence of expectation, the wild cheers bursting simultaneously from eighty thousand tongues, and echoing to the farthest outskirts of the city, the rapid alternations of the fray, the deeds of splendid courage that were manifested, were all well fitted to entrance the imagination. The crimes and servitude of the gladiator were for a time forgotten in the blaze of glory that surrounded him. Representing to the highest degree the courage which the Romans deemed the first of virtues, the cynosure of countless eyes, the chief object of conversation in the metropolis of the universe, destined, if victorious to be immortalised in the mosaic and the sculpture, he not infrequently rose to heroic grandeur. . . . Beautiful eyes, trembling with passion, looked down upon the fight, and the noblest ladies of Rome, even the empress herself, had been known to crave the victor's love.

If Lecky (yes, it was Lecky who wrote that paragraph) could be so excited by the imagined spectacle, who can blame Julia for enjoying the reality?

Julia was ever ready with witty repartee. As to her youthful companions, she replied to her reproving father: "They'll be old one day—with me". When chidden for being a bit too royal, so unlike her father, she replied: "He forgets that he's Caesar: I always remember that I'm Caesar's daughter." She did, too. She was snobbish and very proud of her ancestry of which she often talked, having little else to talk about. She was beautiful, though the early greying of her hair gave her concern. To quote Balsdon's *Roman Women* again:

> She clung, like any other sensible woman, to her youth. She was not very old when her hair started to go grey. One day— the act was typical of him—Augustus came on her as her servants were plucking out her white hairs. He said nothing at all at the time, but some days later this conversation took place:
> *Augustus:* Would you rather be bald or white-haired?
> *Julia:* White-haired, of course.
> *Augustus:* Why then are your servants at such pains to make you bald?
> There is a dreadful probability about it as conversation.

With Agrippa, Julia had found a certain happiness. She realised what a genius he was, even if he was not well-born, and was aged forty to her sixteen. She went abroad with him on his official journeys, she narrowly escaped drowning in the Scamander (which had the cachet of being a very upper-class river, mentioned in Homer), and she was hailed as a goddess in various Asian cities. She bore him five children, a rare feat of productivity in that age and society.

Julia's quips, which suited the taste of Rome's 'slang set', were still being repeated four centuries later, which is how we come to know of them, from the *Saturnalia* of Macrobius, a contemporary of the austere Saint Jerome.

One day, dressed in her primmest gown, she saluted her father

a) Tiberius

b) Agrippina the Elder, the wife of Tiberius

c) Caligula. The two faces of a coin of Caius Caesar Augustus Germanicus

d) Caligula

a) Messalina, the third wife of Claudius, and her children

b) Claudius

c) Agrippina the Younger, the fourth wife of Claudius

with assumed modesty. On the evening before, he had been shocked at her revealing frock, but had said nothing. When he now complimented his daughter on her decorous costume, she answered; "Last night I dressed for my husband, this morning for my father"—a nicely barbed dart for both Augustus and Livia.

Her evening parties were admittedly raffish. She roistered in the Forum, and got drunk on the Rostra, the very shrine, by day, of sycophantic cant and holy humbug. It was rather like holding a cocktail party in the chamber of the House of Commons. They hung garlands on improper statues.

For ten years after Agrippa's death, all went well with Julia, her father, despite his timorous prudery, finding it hard to chasten her. Macrobius tells us:

> Time and again, with a mixture of indulgence and seriousness, her father had suggested that she should behave less extravagantly and choose quieter friends; yet when he reflected on his numerous grandchildren, all of whom took so closely after their father Agrippa, he was ashamed to think of his daughter as anything but a faithful wife. So he lulled himself into imagining that for all her gaiety and her outward flouting of the conventions, she was innocent, and he used to tell his friends that he had two children whose idiosyncrasies he must humour— the Roman government and his daughter. (Tr. Balsdon.)

Julia had entertained lovers during Agrippa's lifetime. Her best-known quip admits it. When one of her *louche* friends went so far as to ask her how it was that, given her way of life, she contrived that her offspring so clearly resembled her husband, she blandly answered that she never took a passenger aboard unless the vessel was already carrying cargo.

In 2 BC the end came. Julia was in her thirty-eighth year, that is by Roman gauges on the threshold of old age. Augustus, when at last he was forced to face the truth, did so with hysterical harshness. Instead of being relegated to a country retreat, Julia was banished to the island of Pandateria, now Ventotene, thirty-one miles west of Naples. Her loyal mother Scribonia went with her.

Rome was aghast, not only because it was losing its most scintillating ornament, but because everyone knew that Augustus would not have been so intemperate as he was if Julia's offence had been merely moral. That there were political overtones was obvious from the downfall of Julia's 'lovers', one a Gracchus, another an Appius Claudius, a third a Cornelius Scipio, a fourth Iullus Antonius, son of Mark Antony who had married a niece of Augustus. When Augustus declared that fire and water would mix sooner than his daughter be reinstated, Romans chucked firebrands into the Tiber. Augustus gave way, or half way. Julia was allowed to dwell in Reggio di Calabria, as it now is, but the ban on wine and even possessing her own property, of which her absentee husband Tiberius, had requested the repeal, was maintained.

Julia lived until AD 14, the year in which her unfeeling father also died, the year in which her former husband Tiberius succeeded. What ruins of lives lay around her. Both her promising sons, Lucius and Gaius, were dead, Lucius in AD 2, Gaius two years later. Agrippa Postumus was banished: he had insulted the Augusta. Julia the Younger had been banished too, because like her mother she had indulged in what Philemon Holland calls 'lewd pranks'. Her downfall involved that of the poet Ovid. He was packed off to Tomi on the Black Sea. What his real offence was we do not know. (The fascination of so many Roman questions lies in the fact that we shall never know the answers to them.) That left only Agrippina. She too would be fruitful and unhappy.

By the time he died, Augustus had lost two grandchildren; a third grandson, his daughter and granddaughter were banished. he had perforce been compelled to adopt Tiberius as his heir and successor.

What a fabric he had built, what a family he had ruined. Livia had had a hand in both. Tacitus gives story after story of her senile and mischievous interference in politics. With all her virtues, which were exemplary, Livia was sullied by what Sallust, and Saint Augustine after him, called the besetting sin of Rome, *libido dominandi*, her lust for power. She was above suspicion save in this one respect. If only she could have forgotten the great days, forgotten her enmity with Tiberius, with Vipsania, with Julia! She could not, and that is why we must pity her. "Old men forget", that is their misfortune. Old women never do: that is ours.

CHAPTER III

Daughters of Dusk

WHEN AUGUSTUS DIED, men realised that the monarchy, by whatever name men cared to call it, had come to stay. Few minded that. True, a few 'republicans' lived on, with something of the cachet which Papists enjoyed under the Hanoverians. As long as they did not cause trouble, they were tolerated, with the vital difference that, for Rome's 'republicans', there would be no 1829: by the end of the first century the very idea was dead.

When, therefore, Tiberius succeeded, in very few breasts did his absolutism rankle. But his behaviour disgusted almost everyone: it was what Tacitus calls his *saevitia*, his bloody-mindedness, that alienated them. The palace up there on the hill was dark and deserted, as it was to remain throughout the new reign. The twice-divorced Tiberius had constructed a vast pleasure-dome, but had installed no empress in it. How in-furiating it was to imagine what this construction might have housed. If only either of Tiberius' wives had been there to run it! But they were not only divorced but dead as well. Julia died in the year of Tiberius' accession in 14, still in harsh banishment aged only fifty-three. Even as crown princess, what a difference she would have made, what warmth she might have kindled, beneath the chilling and ever-lengthening shadow of the aging Augusta. Vipsania, her predecessor, was married to Asinius Gallus to whom she bore five children. She lived until AD 20. Either of them, said the Romans, would have adorned the Palatine, though in very different styles; but neither gaiety nor respectability was that palace to know, only darkness.

As though to vindicate the spite of Rome's smart set, Tiberius'

great palace is almost wholly submerged beneath the lovely
gardens, which, after belonging to the Farnese—they were among
the first botanical gardens in Europe—and then to (of all people)
Napoleon III, now provide amenity for lovers of every nationality.

No wonder Rome was annoyed. Things were even worse
after 27, when Tiberius abandoned Rome for ever. He retired
to the island of Capri, which had the double advantage of being
set in one of the world's most beautiful bays, and of having only
one accessible landing-place. Tiberius used on occasion to creep
up the Tiber, or the Appian Way, to within sight of his capital,
but he never re-entered it. Down in Capri, said the ladies, if he
had no wife, it was quite clear what he was up to, or down to.
Even the Loeb edition of Suetonius cannot bring itself to describe
his frolics in English. The reason seems to be (and it is chastely
flattering to Britannia) that he enjoyed himself not only on dry
land but in and under the water. Out of deference to the moral
integrity of English and American sailors (and to the compassing
sea of Queen Victoria which her Laureate categorised as 'in-
violate') subaqueous sex is deemed to be untranslatable.

More and more the fading emperor left the conduct or mis-
conduct of affairs in the soiled and soiling hands of an upstart
favourite called Sejanus. In the very year of his retirement he sent
out as governor—Procurator he was called—of a third-rate
province, Judaea, a nobody called Pontius Pilate. He must have
obtained the job through Sejanus, 'Caesar's Friend' as he was
politely known. Sejanus fell in 31, and became in a matter of
hours, in Juvenal's biting phrase 'Caesar's enemy' to the fickle
mob, who loyally insulted his corpse as it lay on the bank of
the Tiber. The Jewish intelligence web was then, as it still is, one
of the most sensitive going, and it was the taunt that Pilate would
no longer rank as 'Caesar's Friend' that caused him, against his
better judgment, to condemn Jesus of Nazareth to death.

To be rid of Tiberius was one thing; but who was to succeed
him? So many possibles were dead. Both the grandsons of Augustus were dead, which was why, as he churlishly wrote in his will,
he had made Tiberius his heir. Dead too was Tiberius' brother
Drusus, and Tiberius' son of the same name. The most important
of all, Prince Charming Germanicus, whom Tiberius had been
compelled to adopt as the rival of his own son—Germanicus,
grandson both of Augustus and Augusta, grandson of Mark
Antony had died in the year 10 at Antioch. He was convinced

that he had been poisoned by the governor of Syria, Piso. So was his wife Agrippina I. She was desolated. Her mother, Julia, had never been the wife of a reigning emperor, but would not she, Agrippina, be a Caesar's wife, and dominate the Palatine? No, not now. Her son Gaius, better known by his nickname, Caligula, would be an emperor, her grandson (Nero) too; but posthumous consolation is no prize at all. She loathed Tiberius, who returned her hatred. She never dissembled her dislike of him: how could she? Once when she went to dinner with him she ostentatiously refused an apple he offered her, so as to give the impression she thought it was poisoned—as Tiberius intended she should. He had once before thrown at her a line from a Greek poet which ran: "Do you think you are injured, if you are not suffered to rule?" It was only too true, that was just what she did think. She had produced nine children, of whom six survived. Tiberius did all he could to extinguish them and their mother, to prevent her even from breeding again. When, in 26, this ardent lady wanted to re-marry, he refused her permission. Even in those days there was an unwritten royal marriages act. Two years later, she was arrested and banished to the same island which had been her mother Julia's jail. She was brutally treated. One of her jailers beat her so viciously as to knock out one of her eyes. When she sought death by starvation, her mouth was prized open and food stuffed into it. Tiberius beguiled the two elder of his small grandsons into making indiscreet complaints about his treatment of them. They were duly pronounced public enemies, and they too were doomed to death. Young Nero (not of course the future emperor) was packed off to the island of Ponza. When he beheld the executioner arrive, equipped with the noose for strangling him, and the hook to drag his body to ignominious exposure, he took his own life. He was twenty-five. His brother Drusus, two years older, was confined in a dungeon in the palace, and starved. He even tried to eat the stuffing of his mattress, and so died. The remains of both princes were scattered to the winds.

Only against Gaius, the youngest of Agrippina's three surviving sons, did Tiberius fear to take action. He was already regarded as the embodiment of his father, the new Germanicus, the darling of the troops. He had been on active service with his parents as a child. He had been dressed in army uniform, with army boots, whence his nickname Caligula, *caliga* being a kind of half-Wellington: "little Puss in Boots" might be a modern equivalent.

Tiberius died in the year 37, not on the island of Capri, but at Misenum, the northern headland of the Bay of Naples, where the remains of the imperial palace still excite our admiration. Young Gaius, who was then twenty-five, was suspected of having hastened Tiberius' death by smothering him with a pillow, or by actually strangling him. Both stories were current. An ex-slave who cried out in horror at the deed was at once crucified. Gaius then accompanied the corpse to Rome clad in deep mourning.

From first to last the sentimentality of the Roman legions was far more conspicuous than their loyalty. Young Gaius had been an epileptic. He was prematurely bald, he had sunken eyes and hollow temples. And yet all along the route he was greeted with cries of 'star', 'chicken', 'pet' and similar endearments.

On reaching Rome, Gaius was hailed by the Senate and the populace. He gave Tiberius a magnificent funeral and deposited the ashes in the family mausoleum. He sped away to the islands of Pandateria (now Ventotene) and Ponza to bring back the ashes of his mother and brother (or as much of them as could be recovered), with every possible pomp. By a single decree of the Senate he heaped on his grandmother Antonia all the honours that Augusta had enjoyed, most of which she modestly declined. She died within six weeks of Gaius' accession; but she was an important link in the dynastic chain, because she was the daughter of the famous Mark Antony by his marriage with Augustus' saintly sister Octavia. Gaius Caligula had the great advantage in Roman eyes of being the first ruler to be (a) the direct descendant of Augustus: the line went Scribonia (his first wife)—Julia—Agrippina—Gaius; (b) the direct descendant of Livia Augusta: via Drusus (Tiberius' brother)—Antonia—Germanicus—Gaius; and (c) grandson of Mark Antony, Augustus' competitor for supremacy. In Gaius, therefore, all rivalries were deemed to be buried, unity of blood and destiny embodied.

Agrippina must have been aware of this destiny. It was obvious to one and all, not least to the charming and raffish Jewish prince then living in Rome, a grandson of Herod the Great called Agrippa. He was the favourite of Antonia, and tutor to Tiberius' grandson. He eventually became king of Judaea. He had some narrow scrapes, and was actually imprisoned by Tiberius for being

too outspoken a backer of Gaius. But his family flair for spotting
winners was impeccable: he knew that Gaius must be the next
ruler.

Who was to be the next Cæsar's wife? That was the great
question. The Augusta had died in AD 29, eight long years ago.
Who now was to have the dustsheets removed, the torches
rekindled, and the music strike up once more in the palace on
the hill? Who was to be the favoured (though hardly fortunate)
lady? Everyone guessed that the nuptial couch would be no bed
of roses. Gaius was known to have lived in incest with his sisters,
especially Drusilla. After all, the Ptolemies, conforming to
Egyptian precedent, had done it, so why should he be prudishly
non-conformist? He had been married to a lady called Julia
Claudilla, a noblewoman whose father he drove to suicide.
We hear no more of his daughter. Gaius' next bride was in fact
the bride of someone else, Gaius Pisco. Caligula honoured the
wedding with his presence and then ordered that the lady,
Livia Crestilla, be carried not to Piso's house but to his own.
He divorced her a few days later. She, poor thing, was banished.
His third venture was called Lollia Paulina. She didn't last long
either. His fourth and last wife may well have felt a bit queasy
about her marriage, even if it did make her an empress. She had
by now a good deal to compete with, not only incest, but boys as
well. There was in particular young Mnester, a ballet-dancer, and
a handsome lad called Valerius Catullus who (later on no doubt)
used to claim that he had pleasured Gaius, and that the imperial
demands had quite worn him out. Not satisfied with concubines,
such as Pyrallis, Gaius used to pick and choose among the wives
of his dinner-guests, retiring with the one of his choice and then
handing her back to her husband with (as Suetonius delicately
puts it) visual evidence of their goings-on.

So Caesonia, as the final mate was called, must have known
what she was in for. When Gaius married her, she already had
three daughters by a former marriage. But she was a romp, and
reckoned that the game was worth the candle however brief it
might be. We do not know what she looked like, but we can
at least imagine her coiffure. Saint Peter in his first Epistle (iii, 3)
tells his female flock to avoid 'plaited hair'. The Augusta had
a very long plait, starting at her forehead and then going right
over the top of her head to be wound into a bun at the back.
Agrippina II wore a variation of this. So, even more remarkably,

did the goddess Isis, as shown in the statue in the Naples Museum. Isis was a very fashionable deity, and so it was only natural that she should have been given an imperial hair-style, as natural as that Raphael should depict his Madonnas in the guise of his human inspirers.

Caesonia must have been a charmer. "Although she was neither beautiful nor young," says Suetonius, "besides being a reckless spendthrift and a wanton, Gaius loved her more passionately and more faithfully than any of the others." He liked to tease her. When he'd condemned forty men to death in one morning, he told her at luncheon what a good morning's work he'd done, just to let her know what he could do. Again, he once fondled her with the endearing comment: "I'd even resort to torture to find out why I love you so much." Caesonia would have loved being empress, you might think, more than she loved the emperor. The strange thing about this almost unknown and unhappy enigma is that she loved both. She would go out riding with him in military array, cloak, helmet, shield and all. Of an evening, she would appear naked at dinner. She was a persevering type. She was determined to get her Gaius, and get him she did. She was determined to be empress, and not just another concubine. On the very day she bore him a daughter, she induced Gaius to marry her. The child was called Julia Drusilla, as royal as you could wish. Gaius carried the babe around all the temples, finally confiding her to the care of Minerva, in whose lap he laid her. Naturally enough people wondered whether Gaius really was the father. "Oh yes", he replied, "She must be my daughter, just look what a temper she has: watch her scratching the faces and eyes of her cradle-mates: that's my daughter all right."

Unfortunately the chapters of Tacitus' *Annals* which described Caligula are lost to us. We have Suetonius, and also Josephus, the great Jewish historian, to tell us of his last hours, and those of poor Caesonia too.

After nearly four years, Rome had had enough of Caligula and his pathological beastliness. A plot to kill him was headed by a soldier who had risen from the ranks to become a colonel of the Guards. Caligula had publicly insulted him, making obscene gestures implying that Chaerea, for such was his name, was a passive homosexual. In the winter of the year 41, Caligula had decided to hold a four-day festival in honour of Augustus. Already he had decided that he was himself divine, and besides insulting the Jews, for whom Herod Agrippa very bravely and successfully stood up, had designed a bridge which was to link the Palatine with the Capitol, that is the two divinities Caligula and Jupiter. For the celebration, amid all the diverse building-materials, and in front of the great brick terrace, which he had added to the palace, temporary galleries had been erected. Here the populace were accommodated without any regard to rank or proper surveillance. On the last day of the exercises Caligula retired for luncheon about mid-day. Because of his building mania the whole region was in disorder and security had lapsed. In one of those still dank and sinister corridors which lead up from the Forum to the Palatine, Chaerea awaited his prey. Caligula stopped to talk with some boys whom he had summoned from Greece and Ionia, ostensibly to sing the hymn composed in his honour. There and then he was killed by Chaerea and his accomplices, some taking care to thrust their daggers through the pudenda of their epicene lord. His end was as squalid as it was deserved. The sequel was horrible. His German bodyguard ran amok, cutting down anyone they met. The citizenry panicked. The conspirators who had no more idea of how to realise 'liberty' than those on whom they had modelled themselves, the assassins of Julius Caesar in 44 BC, dispersed and hid. But they had determined that Caesonia must die too. Some held her innocent, but it was generally believed that she was Caligula's evil genius. He was known to be besotted with her, so much so that it was said she had procured his passion by the administration of an over-powerful aphrodisiac which had driven him out of his wits—a typically sleazy piece of Roman gossip which both Juvenal and Josephus repeat. An executioner was accordingly despatched to kill her. He was called Lupus, the Wolf. He found her in the deserted palace lying by Gaius' body, which was sprawled on the ground. She was smeared with the blood from his wounds. Their little daughter Julia, Minerva's nursling, was there too. Caesonia was moaning in distraught lamentation, in half-heard words which bewailed her lost husband. Was she reproaching him for being too harsh, or for not heeding her warnings? No one would ever know. The poor woman was hysterical. Lupus was shaken with embarrassment at this awful sight. He was plainly unwilling to play the lethal part for which he had been so unexpectedly cast. It was Caesonia who triumphed. "Come here," she said, rising from the ground. She then deliberately stretched forth her neck, and so met her end. Little Julia was butchered too, one account says by having her head dashed against the wall.

So ended Caesonia, a gallant gambler in life, brave in death, and of all the Caesars' wives the one of whom we know the least, except that she knew how to love even the least lovable of men; and that is an epitaph worth having.

CHAPTER IV

Messalina

WITH THE MURDER of Gaius-Caligula in 41, it might well
seem that the knell of the Julio-Claudians had at last been
sounded. Rome was in turmoil. No one knew what was to be
done, what might happen; no one that is except Herod Agrippa
(not that he ever used the name Herod in Rome: 'Agrippa' the
friend of Augustus, father of Agrippina I, after whom he had been
named, sounded better). As soon as Claudius, Germanicus'
younger brother, was dragged into the waning winter light from
behind the curtain in the palace where he had been skulking,
Agrippa realised that the dynasty not only could, but must,
go on. Continuity in Rome as in Jerusalem was the only guarantee
of stability. His own family history had taught him that. So,
largely through the intervention of this expert and persuasive
manipulator, Claudius became emperor. The pathetic, doltish
don, now aged 51 like his friend from Palestine, shoved into
eminence by an oriental friend, promoted to stardom by a Jewish
charmer—the story sounds as though it belongs to Los Angeles
in the 1920s. It actually was acted out in Rome of the AD 40s.

Gibbon, in one of his slyest footnotes (Ch. iii), tells us that
"we may remark that of the first fifteen emperors, Claudius was
the only one whose taste in love was entirely correct." This
entire correctness embraced two of the most famous murderesses
in history.

Claudius had started early. He was twice betrothed before
being married. As his first wife he wed Plautia Urganilla, the
granddaughter of one of Livia Augusta's cronies. She came of a
well-bred, but rather wild Etruscan family. (Her brother rid

himself of his wife by throwing her out of the window. He
pleaded, vainly, that it was sleep-walking.) Claudius, always
timid, divorced Plautia. They had two children, both of whom died
in infancy, the boy from an accident. He was choked by a pear
which he had tossed and caught in his open mouth. Claudius
disowned the girl on the ground that he was not her father.
Next came Aelia Paetina, who gave birth to a daughter and was
then discarded. Who was to be the third? One of the entrants
was actually Lollia Paulina, Caligula's cast-off. In the end,
largely through the intrigues of court slaves and civil servants,
the emperor's hand and bed went to Valeria Messalina. She
was a gay, good-looking girl of excellent family, when at the
age of fourteen she was married to Claudius who was forty-eight.
By the time of Claudius' accession in 41, they had been married
about a year. They had two children, a daughter born just before
Claudius' elevation called Octavia who was one day to marry
Nero, and a son just a year later, called Britannicus. Nero would
in due course murder them both. Murder ran in the family,
Unfortunately, the missing chapters of Tacitus include the first
six years of Claudius' reign. We start off in the seventh with a
typical intrigue of Messalina's. Everyone in Rome knew her by
this time for the whore she was, everyone that is except her imperial and myopic husband.

Here any writer on Roman affairs must enter a *cavaet*.
Tacitus says at the outset of his *Annals*, that he will write
'without resentment or bias'. He does not always do so; but
how many historians do? What is a writer to include or
discard? Pliny's rule (and he was by no means the first to define it)
was that it is a writer's duty to narrate, not to judge. In dealing
with Roman history this is of particular importance. Tacitus,
Suetonius and Dio all relate scandalous details about leading
Romans, and their vices. But how can we be justified in dismissing
a story of sexual licence as 'gossip', and then accept as fact one
of murder on the next page? It seems more honest to give the
tale as it is told. After all, modern memoirs have given us unsavoury but authentic examples of lubricity in characters hitherto
regarded as unblemished.

When Tacitus' story begins again, Claudius has been emperor
for six years, and Messalina is firmly in the saddle. When she
cast about for a new lover it was always she who made the
running. And she really did love them, until she tired of them.

Polybius, a high court official, was killed in 47. Caligula's sister Julia Livilla, and Seneca, her alleged bedmate, were both banished, Livilla for the second time.

The crisis was brought on by Poppaea Sabina, 'the most beautiful woman of her age' and older than Messalina which was so galling. Poppaea had filched Messalina's current lover, a handsome ballet-dancer called Mnester. "Mnester had been unwilling to accommodate her at first; but Messalina cajoled Claudius, under the impression that she needed his help in some worthy cause, into sending him an order that he 'was to obey Messalina'. To disobey this mandate would have meant death. Mnester had formerly been on intimate terms with Caligula, so when he gave his command performance with Messalina she was so grateful to him that she made him leave the stage and live in her house. The public were offended at being deprived of its favourite dancer. Messalina went further. When Claudius called in all the copper currency bearing Caligula's head, she contrived to get hold of it, and have it melted down to furnish the material for statues of Mnester.

Messalina thought out what at first sight seemed a highly ingenious plan, which was going to kill two birds with one stone. It killed more than two, including Messalina herself. The scheme was to eliminate Poppaea without incriminating Mnester.

It happened that the famous Gardens of Lucullus, on the Pincio near the Trinita dei Monti, were at that time in the possession of a rich and highly respected man who had twice been consul and was a keen horticulturist. His name was Asiasticus. The gardens were the finest in Rome. Messalina wanted them. She also wanted to keep Mnester. She therefore instructed one of her creatures, called Suillius (a man of the lowest reputation, who had been banished for corruption, but was now back) to poison Claudius' mind against Asiaticus. To make the manœuvre look more decent, Sosibius, young Britannicus' tutor, was to be his accomplice. Sosibius therefore told Claudius that Asiaticus had sinister designs on Claudius, and had boasted of having been one of Caligula's assassins. This was untrue: he had merely remarked that he wished he had been. Claudius had had Caligula's real assassins put to death, because if people started killing Caesars, how safe would he be? Without more ado, Claudius summoned Rufrius Crispus, the commander of the Guard,

and sent him off to Baiae "with an army large enough to crush
a rebellion", as Tacitus puts it. So Asiaticus, this man who had
held two consulships, was brought back to Rome in chains. He
was not allowed to appeal to the Senate. He was tried in a bedroom, with Messalina there.

He behaved with silent dignity, while the usual fictitious
charges were made—bribery, corruption and adultery with Poppaea
Sabina. Effeminacy was added for good measure. At this point
Asiaticus found his voice: "Ask your sons, Suillius: they will
testify to my masculinity." Claudius was much moved during
the trial, especially when one of Asiaticus' friends said how
well the ex-consul had fought against the British. Even Messalina
cried a bit, or pretended to. She left the bedroom as though to
dry her tears, but actually to send someone to order Poppaea to
kill herself. Terrified by Messalina's threats, she took her own life.

Asiaticus was condemned. He died as he had lived, with
dignity. He bathed and supped as usual, and ordered his
funeral pyre to be moved a little to the side, so as not to injure
his trees. He then opened his veins, that being the most favoured
method of committing compulsory suicide, when, as is this case,
the victim, as a special favour, was allowed to choose his form
of death. How much did Claudius know about all this? Apparently
not much, for when, a few days later, Poppaea's husband was
dining with the emperor, Claudius asked him why he hadn't
brought his wife. "She's dead," was the truthful and tactful
reply.

Messalina was now at the apex of her power. She was accorded
the privilege of driving through Rome in a carriage and pair,
a favour normally accorded only to the Vestal Virgins and a few
very exalted priestesses. The rest had to walk, or be carried in
a chair or litter.

Rufrius did well out of the plot. He was made an honorary
praetor, and given two-and-a-half million sesterces. Sosibius
received another million. Suillius went on with his murder
campaign.

Like Julia before her, Messalina enjoyed night-life. It was said
that she covered her black hair with a flaxen wig and practised
under the name Lycisca in a dingy down-town brothel. The wig
may well have been made of German tresses, which were imported
into the capital. Most Romans then as now were dark-haired,
but, like other races, have often shown a preference for blondes.

Such is the story as told by Juvenal and Pliny. Dio published a more refined version: the empress set up a brothel in the palace, to where only real ladies were admitted. Decorum was preserved; they had to bring their husbands, who acted as procurers.

The satire in which Juvenal pillories Messalina is one of the most fascinating essays on woman ever devised, so fascinating in fact that until quite recently school editions of Juvenal, even in Australia, simply omitted it altogether. In our own generation it still strikes the reader as being exhaustively frank. There are two modern translations of it. The first was issued in a limited edition by the Casanova Society in 1926, entitled *Woman, a Satire, from the Latin of Juvenal, with an introduction by F. D. Wright*. It is done into elegant heroic couplets. Here are two samples:

> But all the world from furthest East to West
> Knows well how Clodius as a flute-girl dressed,
> Showed the assembled dames a phallus lewd
> Huger than two of Caesar's *Anti-prude*. [Supposed title
> of one of Caesar's 'works'.]

> In any house where dwells a catamite,
> Whose quivering fingers to lewd joy invite,
> You'll find the lord and lady are the same
> As that base wretch, and practise his foul game.

The second version is available to all, as a London Panther book—*The Satires of Juvenal*, a new verse translation by Charles Plumb, 1968. The celebrated Sixth is entitled 'The Ladies—God damn 'em'. It is so racy that it seems contemporary. As such, it causes more surprise to us than the original did to the Romans of Juvenal's day. And for a simple reason. Nowadays most youngsters acquire their first inklings of sex, their first intimations of immorality, not from substance but from shadows, from media of communication which interpose, quite literally, a film between reality and cognition. In the ancient world that was not so. Fact came before fiction; experience was the norm, not succedaneous frustration. Juvenal's satire therefore is not to be regarded as a guide to evil, as 'tending to deprave or corrupt'. It is simply a witty, corrosive commentary on, not an introduction to, real life.

It analyses every folly of which woman is capable. All the types are there. The nymphomaniac, the alcoholic, the termagant, the political dame, the climber, the learned lady. Cosmetics are ridiculed, and hair-styles (which helps us to date the work, because Juvenal's hair-castles which demanded a front view only, leaving madam bald at the back, flourished only in the early days of the emperor Hadrian, say in the second and third decade of the second century). Every possible variation of debauchery is denounced, even to purported advice on eunuchs, how to choose them, and at what age to have them merit the name.

That this world did exist is beyond doubt, despite prim editors; and it is into this world that Juvenal introduces Messalina, candidly and convincingly.

To celebrate the eighth centenary of the city's foundation in the year 47, Claudius decided to revive the Secular Games. They had last been given by Augustus sixty-four years ago. These were attended by little Britannicus, Claudius' son, now in his sixth year, and by little Nero, who was about twelve. It was Nero who received the most applause, partly because he was the only surviving male descendant of Germanicus; but even at this early age he must have possessed something of that deceptive charm which was to ruin him and so many others. Besides, people were so sorry for his mother, whom Messalina now persecuted with unremitting venom. But Messalina had already gone too far. She was bored by mere adultery and so as Tacitus puts it "she drifted into unfamiliar vices". Her final drift was indeed 'unfamiliar'.

She had fixed her lascivious gaze on a man called Gaius Silius, and he had been her paramour for at least twelve months. He was the handsomest man in Rome, and consul designate for the next year, 48. No doubt he owed his advancement to Messalina. He was only thirty-two, the same age as Agrippina II. Most men had to wait ten years longer for a consulship. His family achieved eminence under Augustus, and in little more than half a century had produced five consuls and been made patrician. Gaius' father had been the friend of Germanicus and of his wife Agrippina I. He commanded the army in Upper Germany for seven years, from 14 to 21, but fell a victim to Tiberius' malevolence and was forced to commit suicide. Silius the younger was married to an aristocratic wife Junia Silana. He was a polished orator, and he was ambitious. Messalina forced him to divorce

Agrippina the Younger, from the bust in the Naples Museum

a) Nero—the youthful artist as the Greeks saw him, and as he saw himself. From Corinth

b) Nero

c) Vespasian

his Junia. She wanted him all to herself. He was her prize; but her success proved the death-warrant of them both. Silius fully appreciated the danger of being caught in Messalina's golden web; but to refuse her advances would have meant certain death. Why then should they wait until Claudius was dead, why not get married at once? Their liaison was no secret. Messalina came to Silius' house with a troop of followers, she clung to him when they went out, and his mistress heaped wealth and honours on him. The emperor's slaves and ex-slaves, even his family heirlooms were to be found in the adulterer's house. In the end "you really might have thought that the empire had changed hands". Silius may be excused for thinking that, *de facto*, it already had, so why not make the transition *de jure*, by a marriage? "Your power," he told Messalina, "will remain undiminished. I have no children and I'm ready to adopt Britannicus. Peace of mind will only be yours if we forestall Claudius. He is slow to discover deception, but quick to anger."

Messalina at first was unreceptive. She had no love for her old husband, but she feared that Silius, once supreme, might despise his mistress. She may well have been right. But in the end she gave in. "The idea of being called his wife appealed to her by its sheer outrageousness—a sensualist's ultimate satisfaction." so she agreed to Silius' plan. The wedding duly took place, formally and officially solemnised. Silius was exhilarated. He knew that 'in delay there lies no plenty', and that even with the odds so long, he might bring off a coup which would exalt him to the summit, because his marriage would make him, when Claudius died, stepfather to Britannicus, who was the legitimate heir to the purple.

The palace clique were horrified. Mnester had been no menace to them, but Silius was. Inevitably if he became the husband of the empress, he would be the ruler and out they would be thrown. Lover? yes, but husband no. That was how they saw it. Claudius saw nothing. Always more interested in public works than in private morals, he was down at Ostia. He had gone there to supervise the grain supply, and to attend a religious ceremony. He had prolonged his stay, because he was anxious to inspect his grand new harbour, begun two years earlier, with its twin curving breakwaters, and the great mole in front. The foundation of the mole was the hull of the ship which had brought to Caligula from Egypt the obelisk which now adorns the piazza in front

E

of St Peter's in Rome. The harbour came into being so that the grain-ships from Egypt could be safely and speedily unloaded. Grain shortages in Rome were apt to lead to riots. During one of them Claudius himself had been pelted in the Forum.

Meanwhile up in Rome, Messalina had been contriving a few useful murders, which included that of Claudius' own son-in-law and his parents, so that Claudius' daughter might be free to marry her own half-brother. That had been at the beginning of this fateful year. It was now autumn and the vintage was in full swing. Messalina, as the possessor both of Silius and her coveted gardens, decided to hold a frolic in them. It was to take the form of a mimic antique grape-harvest. The wine-presses were at work, new wine was filling the vats to overflowing, while a group of women clad as Maenads capered round them. Messalina led the orgy, with her hair streaming, and a Bacchic wand in her hand. Silius, the consul-designate, wore a wreath of ivy on his brow and buskins on his feet. He lolled his head in tune with the rest. One guest—they were all drunk by now—climbed a tall tree. What can you see from up there? he was asked. A storm over Ostia, he replied with some wit. The storm was soon to break over Rome.

Narcissus, one of the ex-slaves who had contrived the death of Silius' father, took the lead. He convinced the other ex-slaves at court that none of them was safe: had not the murdered Polybius been one of themselves? Some of his côterie were for delay. Narcissus knew that it must be now or never, because Claudius was so susceptible that he might relent if he was given time. Narcissus therefore induced two of Claudius' favourite concubines to turn informer, and to tell the imperial cuckold just what had been going on in Rome while his back was turned. Narcissus was summoned. When Claudius asked him to tell him the whole disreputable story, this astute rogue said he would make no reference to the past, only to the present. "I merely want to ask Caesar one simple question. Are you aware that you are divorced?" At last Claudius understood. He ordered his carriage, and set out for Rome. The news was soon all over the City. Messalina and Silius separated. The whole party panicked. Messengers and rumours kept pouring in: Claudius would soon be back, on vengeance bent. Although Claudius' most intimate friends had confirmed the concubines' allegation, Narcissus took the precaution of travelling in the same carriage as the

emperor, knowing how easily he might change his mind if
Messalina got at him. Dazed and infuriated, Claudius kept on
asking, "Am I still emperor? Is Silius still a private citizen?"

Messalina did exactly what Narcissus had foreseen. She sent
urgent messages to Octavia and Britannicus to intercede with
their father. Messalina even approached the Senior Vestal
Virgin, Vibidia. Then from her gardens, she walked through the
city with only three companions for of course all the sycophants
had deserted her and gone into hiding. Many of them were soon
caught and punished. When the pathetic little quartet reached
the Ostian Gate, they found a rubbish-cart and begged a lift.
When they met the returning emperor, Messalina behaved as
Narcissus had anticipated. She cried a good deal, and said that
Claudius must give a hearing to the mother of Octavia and
Britannicus. Narcissus shouted her down, telling Claudius (who
was in fact wavering) all about the wedding, and handing to
him a long indictment, which catalogued all Messalina's crimes.
Then, as they entered the Gate, along came the children and the
Vestal Virgin. Narcissus had the children led away, but he
could not insult Vibidia the Vestal, who insisted that a wife
should not be killed without trial. Narcissus conceded this, and
then rudely added that Vibidia had better go home and mind her
own holy business. Claudius was dumbfounded. His craven
friend Lucius Vitellius was studiously ambiguous in replying
to any question. Narcissus was now in sole and complete charge.
He assumed command of the Guard. He persuaded Claudius
to go to Silius' house, which was really Claudius' own property,
and inspect it. When they were inside, Narcissus pointed to a
statue of Silius' father which, when he was condemned, should
have been destroyed. And all over the mansion were family
heirlooms of Claudius' own family, the Claudii and the Drusi.

Claudius now fell, as Narcissus had intended, into one of his
blind rages. He was hustled off to the barracks, where he addressed
the garrison with such indignation that they at once demanded
that vengeance should take its course. Silius was brought in. He
made no defence, merely asking that he be put to death quickly.
Poor Silius: he really had been so much more sinned against
than sinning. A number of his associates were summarily
slaughtered, because the whole episode had been treated as a
treason trial. In Rome politics have always come before morals.
The victims included one young man who had enjoyed Messalina

for one night only and had then been discarded. Only Mnester
caused delay. He recalled the emperor's own command, and
claimed that, unlike the others, he had been constrained to do
what he had done. He tore his clothes and showed the weals
on his back left by Messalina's whip. It was to be his last act.
Claudius was inclined to pardon him. But why, asked the clique,
should a dancer live when so many gentlemen had died? So
Mnester met his end. So did many others. One man escaped
because of his uncle's distinguished record of service to the
State, another because at Messalina's vintage party he had
played a female rôle.

Meanwhile up in her lovely ill-gotten gardens, Messalina was
preparing an apologia. She still cherished the hope that she
might prevail. Indeed she might have done, had it not been for
Narcissus. After resting, and being a bit fuddled, Claudius asked
that 'the poor woman' as he called her should present her defence
on the morrow. This was noted. Clearly his anger was waning
and his love waxing. Delay might mean that conjugal relations
would be resumed.

Narcissus darted out. He bade an officer of the Guard,
ostensibly on Claudius' orders, to go and kill Messalina. While
the escort was being assembled, a former slave called Euodos
was sent ahead to prevent her escaping, and to see that the order
was carried out. Arriving at the gardens, he found Messalina
prostrate on the ground, with her mother Domitia Lepida sitting
beside her. When Messalina was all-powerful, they had quarelled,
but now Domitia showed compassion—very Roman compassion. "Wait for the executioner," were her comforting words.
"Your life is finished. All that remains is to make a good end."
Messalina, steeped in vice as she had been for so long, could do
nothing of the sort. She was still moaning frantically when the
execution-squad forced their way in. The officer just stood there.
Euodos reviled her in filthy terms. At last Messalina gave up
hope. She was handed a dagger. She put it to her throat, and then
to her breast; but her hand shook so much that she could not use
it. The silent officer simply ran her through, and left the body
with her mother.

Claudius was still at dinner when the death of Messalina was
announced, whether by her own hand or another's was not made
clear. Claudius did not enquire. He merely asked for more wine
and went on with the party.

Such was the end of this gay, cruel little harlot. It is generally recognised that pornocracy, that is rule by harlots, arrived in Rome in the year 904. At least in this one respect if in no others, Messalina had shown that she could be centuries ahead of her time. She was only twenty-three.

CHAPTER V

Agrippina

THE DEATH OF Messalina caused general consternation. First, among those to whom she had sold offices, had assisted to ill-gotten wealth, or saved from just punishment. They had all reckoned on a long period of enjoyment and peace, with a patroness so young and (as it seemed) so powerful.

Claudius always favoured the adviser he had last heard. To gain time he was induced to inform the praetorians that as his wives had turned out so badly he would remain a widower, and if he did not keep his promise he would not refuse death at their hands. Ominous it was, that this declaration was made to the Guard, not the Senate. The palace clique, being closest to the emperor, realised that their very lives depended on finding a new empress who would leave them to manage the Empire. So they set about choosing one. Claudius presided at this selection committee, and there they sat 'like viziers nodding together in some Arabian Night', for it is to fiction rather than fact that the outcome bears more resemblance. There were three 'starters', all of whom hated each other. Callistus backed Lollia Paulina, who had been Caligula's third wife. Narcissus was all for Aelia Paetina, who had already been Claudius' own second wife. Pallas was promoting Agrippina the younger, daughter of Germanicus and Agrippina the elder. Her pedigree was impeccable. She was descended directly from Augustus, via Julia and Agrippa, on her mother's side, and from Livia, via her son Nero Claudius Drusus and Germanicus, on her father's. She was also through her paternal grandmother lineally descended from Mark Antony, by his marriage with Augustus' sister Octavia. She was Caligula's

sister, and niece of the reigning emperor, Claudius. If the power
and the glory were to be kept within the family, as surely they
ought to be, for the benefit of this corrupt cabal, then Agrippina
was the best candidate. Besides, the child she would bring with
her was the grandson of Germanicus, the boy known as Domitius,
who was fully deserving of imperial rank. This lad was later to
bear the name Nero, and to make it infamous; but it was a name
famous and honoured in Roman annals, because it was a Nero
who in 207 BC had routed the Carthaginian invaders at the battle
of the Metaurus. So in the end they decided that Agrippina it
must be. It turned out to be one of the most disastrous decisions
ever taken—disastrous for the clique, for the family and for Rome.

Agrippina was born in AD 15, so by the year 49 she was
thirty-four, matured, *rusée* and rich. She was very beautiful still.
She had been twice widowed. Her first husband was Gnaeus
Domitius Ahenobarbus, 'Redbeard'—stigmatised by Suetonius
as being 'detestable in every aspect of his life'. Caligula in one
of his madder moods had created his three sisters, all married
women, honorary Vestal Virgins. Agrippina was in fact pregnant.
When in December 37 she gave birth to Nero (it is simpler to
call him that straight away), her odious husband, who had once
deliberately killed a boy by driving over him on the Appian
Way, and had gouged out a man's eye in the Forum, blandly
remarked that any child born to him and Agrippina must be a
monster and a public curse. After the death of Ahenobarbus in
the year 40, Agrippina set her cap at Galba, the future emperor,
even before his wife's death; but Galba's mother-in-law would
have none of it, denounced Agrippina before a company of matrons
and boxed her ears. Agrippina then married Passienus Crispus,
because he was extremely rich. He had previously been married
to Domitia, Nero's aunt, and had then divorced her. Agrippina
was his heir, and he was by her wiles soon despatched. Domitia
naturally enough was Agrippina's enemy for life.

Agrippina, now a rich woman, decided that she could play
for the highest stakes of all—Claudius.

Agrippina is often coupled in the catalogue of infamy with
Messalina. Both, it is true, were vicious, both rapacious, both
murderesses; but there is something grand, a sort of warped
nobility, about Agrippina. Messalina, as Tacitus puts it, just
toyed with politics to satisfy her whimsical lusts. Agrippina
flew much higher. She has a dramatic attraction in the class

of Lady Macbeth. She would have been a wonderful subject for a play by Euripides, the 'most tragic' of Athenian dramatists in Aristotle's estimation. It is all the more fascinating therefore that she became the heroine in a play by a dramatist who admired Euripides to the extent of founding two of his plays on Euripidean drama. Jean Racine was born in 1639. By the age of twenty-one he was already a poetical courtier. He graduated to drama, and in 1669, produced as his fifth play *Britannicus*. It is Aggripina who dominates the piece; but the subject *Britannicus* would appeal to sentiment—the wicked murder of an innocent boy; besides the title had been suggested by a British princess, Henrietta of England, sister-in-law of Louis XIV. Of Racine's eleven tragedies, six bear a woman's name, and in three others, including *Britannicus*, it is a woman who sustains the leading role. The drama, in Voltaire's words, "has all the energy of Tacitus in lines worthy of Virgil . . . the development of Nero's character is a masterpiece." High praise indeed, from a severe critic. But the praise is justified, and the reason for its being justified is simply the stature of the originals.

Agrippina had been born amid the clash of arms and the vicissitudes of war. Her father Germanicus had commanded an army on the Rhine, and it was in his headquarters that Aggrippina first saw the light. Germanicus was charming, but he was not a great general. That title belongs more justly to his mother, Agrippina the elder, daughter of Augustus' minister Agrippa by Julia. She had been manhandled by undisciplined troops, and on another occasion had actually confronted the soldiery and allayed a panic. She was tough and determined. When Germanicus, who had been allowed a triumph for his German exploits, died on active service at Antioch two years later, Agrippina was convinced that he had been poisoned by Piso, governor of Syria. She hastened back to Rome, bearing her husband's ashes. There her plaints caused the arrest of Piso. So common was poisoning in that era that there was a special court for the trial of poison cases. But as this was a matter which concerned the imperial family, Tiberius committed it to the Senate. Piso killed himself. Agrippina and Tiberius were irreconcilable. The sorry tale of her exile and death has already been told.

It was against this background of malice, suspicion and violence that the younger Agrippina grew up. Nor did her prospects brighten when Tiberius' evil adviser Sejanus fell in 31. Few lives in Rome can have been so miserable as that of Agrippina and her young son. Her brother, the emperor Gaius Caligula exiled her while the family were in the north, in the year 39. She was relegated to the island of Ponza; Caligula not only killed her current lover, but compelled her to carry his ashes back to Rome before proceeding to her island prison. Nero, now a child of two, was left behind in Rome, to be brought up in poverty, in the house of his aunt Lepida, by a dancer and a barber, ideal instructors for the real Nero who would later manifest himself.

When Claudius became emperor in 41, Agrippina was recalled, and reinstated. Nero not only recovered his father's property, but was also enriched by a legacy from his stepfather Passienus. It was even rumoured that Messalina would have liked him out of the way, and had sent emissaries to strangle him as he was taking his siesta.

Agrippina was now free to make the highest bid of all—to be empress. Being a niece of Claudius, it was easy for her to establish an affectionate, indeed intimate, relationship with her uncle. She took trouble to look her best, especially when Claudius was in his cups. Pallas was now her lover, and it was he who convinced Claudius that he must marry Agrippina. The only obstacle was a legal impediment; because by Roman law as it then stood, marriage of uncle and niece was accounted incestuous. The Senate was seduced by the arts of Lucius Vitellius, a toadying sycophant with a ready tongue. He suggested to the Senate that their master must have a wife to share his arduous duties; and when the house had warmly applauded this opening gambit, Vitellius proposed Agrippina as the ideal consort. Claudius, who had already assured Vitellius that he would yield to the Senate's recommendation—he was a citizen like anyone else, he said—now appeared. After being congratulated by the throng in the Forum, he entered the Senate and asked them to pass a decree to legalise marriage with a brother's daughter. The marriage of Claudius and Agrippina took place 'with hardly a day's delay'.

Already Agrippina had made dynastic plans. The first step must be the betrothal of her son Nero, now aged twelve, to Claudius' daughter Octavia, who was a few years younger. She was already engaged to another, who with convenient spite committed suicide on the day of the wedding. His sister was banished.

> From this moment [says Tacitus] the country was transformed. Complete obedience was accorded to a woman—and not a woman like Messalina who meddled with national affairs to satisfy her appetites. This was a rigorous, almost masculine despotism. In public, Agrippina was austere and often arrogant. Her private life was chaste—unless power was to be gained. Her passion to acquire money was unbounded. She wanted it as a stepping stone to supremacy.

Caligula had called Livia 'Ulysses in petticoats'. Agrippina coupled the wiles of Ulysses with the vigour of Hercules. Within the year young Nero was adopted by Claudius. This meant that Nero, not his own child Britannicus, was now legally his elder son, and therefore his heir. Naturally there was little love lost between the two lads. Britannicus, however charming he may have been, was tactless. Meeting Nero soon after his adoption, he addressed him as 'Domitius', not as Nero, for it was on his adoption that he had formally taken that name, together with those of Claudius Drusus Germanicus and Caesar.

Agrippina had Seneca recalled from exile in Corsica to be her son's tutor, and had Burrus, a former factor of Livia's, placed in sole command of the Guard. She could now make the unique boast which Racine puts in her mouth that she was daughter, wife, sister and mother of the lords of Rome. She used her authority to the full. She was proclaimed Augusta, the first woman to be thus exalted in her lifetime. She was allowed the official carriage and pair. She was amassing vast wealth for Nero. Murder had become her usual means.

She killed Lollia Paulina because she had been the wife of her brother Caligula and had cherished the hope of marrying Claudius. Dio adds the disgusting detail that when Lollia's head was brought to her, Agrippina did not recognise it. So to make sure, with her own hand she opened the dead woman's mouth and inspected her teeth, which she knew were irregular.

The death of Silanus while betrothed to Octavia has already been recorded. The first husband of Claudius' other daughter, by Aelia Paetina, was stabbed to death in the year 47, while in bed with a favourite boy. Murder was endemic in the court of

Claudius, we must remember, even before the advent of Agrippina. In the palace, she only did what the palace had long been doing. She did not invent the fashion, she followed it; but in addition to fashion, Agrippina had style.

Nero was being brought more and more into the public eye. Britannicus was a palace prisoner. Sosibius was his tutor, but Agrippina soon had him killed, on the pretext that he was plotting against Nero. Britannicus was then handed over to creatures of her own, who did him all the harm they could.

Agrippina often attended the emperor in public, when he was transacting ordinary business or when he was receiving ambassadors, but she sat on a separate tribunal—"one of the most remarkable sights of the time", says Dio. It must have been. Agrippina was now in her late thirties, and knew how to cut a dash. She wore gorgeous clothes, some of them shot with gold thread, such as Dido had woven of old.

She was busily bringing Nero forward, and in as favourable a light as possible. When Claudius fell ill, it was Nero, then about sixteen or seventeen, who was bidden to enter the Senate and promise a horse-race if Claudius recovered. Despite Agrippina's ardent prayers, he did. Then she instigated a riot about the sale of bread, and persuaded Claudius to make a proclamation and to repeat in a letter to the Senate, that if anything happened to him, Nero was quite capable of conducting affairs of state. By such means Nero was built up into a public figure, whereas no one really knew whether Britannicus were still alive. Some regarded him as insane, or epileptic.

Agrippina had all the honours and privileges which Livia had enjoyed. She exercised the same power as Claudius, but she wanted to possess his title outright. Like her predecessor, Livia, she annoyed him by helping to put out a fire in the city. Nero appeared in the circus wearing triumphal regalia. Britannicus was still dressed as a child. People drew the inevitable conclusion.

They reckoned without Claudius. In one of those fits of lucidity which sometimes visited him, he realised that Agrippina was intolerable: he had had five years of her and that was enough. She had destroyed among others Lepida, Messalina's mother who had helped bring up Nero. Titus Statilius Taurus, famous for his wealth and gardens, she had goaded to suicide. It was a question who should stand first in Nero's affection.

Agrippina or his aunt Lepida. Both were rich, both beautiful, and both were immoral, disreputable and violent.

Narcissus had opposed the murder of Domitia, and now plainly discerned what Agrippina was moving towards. He knew that he was doomed. He saw in Agrippina a second Messalina and he became so mentally preoccupied that his health broke down. Her current paramour was still Pallas.

Meanwhile Claudius, like Narcissus, showed more and more favour to Britannicus. It was high time he donned the man's toga, and then he could be proclaimed heir. Agrippina saw that she must act quickly. Narcissus' extremity was her opportunity. She packed him off to Campania, to Sinuessa on the coast north of Naples; it would be good for his gout, she said.

It was generally believed, Suetonius tells us, that Claudius was poisoned. There seems to be no doubt that he was. The great attraction of poison, especially in the days before firearms, was that you could kill without proximity. When you have a dagger in your hand, it is very hard to prove an alibi but it is far easier if you use poison—for preference a slow-acting one. Agrippina therefore called in a professional poisoner called Locusta, a Gallic woman who was already under a sentence of death, so expert had she shown herself. She had a long career of imperial service ahead of her.

Various guesses were made as to how the poison was administered. What is certain is that a mushroom was the vehicle. The date was 12th October of AD 54. It is the date which gives us the best clue. Nowadays, year by year, the Italian newspapers publish, in the autumn, stories of people, sometimes whole families, being killed by eating *funghi*, poisonous toadstools, in the belief that they are mushrooms. When they are cooked the difference is all the harder to tell. All Agrippina had to do was to have one of these poisonous imitations served up in a dish of genuine mushrooms, and, as the story goes, administer it to him 'with her own hand'. Claudius, who was a glutton and was particularly fond of mushrooms, grabbed it, gobbled it up and so died. (See note on page 177).

Agrippina had thought out all the ensuing manœuvres in detail. The death was concealed: prayers were offered for Claudius' safety as though he were ill, and the farce was kept up by bringing in comic actors, under pretence that he had asked to be entertained by them. No one was allowed to leave the palace and all the entrances were guarded. Agrippina, looking heart-broken, drew Britannicus to her, as though deriving comfort from contact with him. He was so like his dear father, she said. He was then confined to his own room. Agrippina kept on issuing cheerful bulletins about Claudius' health, to keep up the army's morale, and to await the propitious hour forecast by the astrologers.

At last, at noon on 13th October, the palace gates were suddeny thrown open. Attended by Burrus, out came Nero to the battalion on duty. He was greeted with cheers, and carried in a litter to the Guards' camp. Some of the troops were bewildered and asked where Britannicus was; but as no one was prepared to reply to that question they fell in with the rest.

Nero made a short allocution to the Praetorians, of which the most important sentence was a promise to reward the troops as lavishly as his father had done. He was then hailed as emperor. The Senate and the provinces duly followed suit. How smoothly it had all gone! Claudius was given a splendid funeral, modelled on that of Augustus. Nero pronounced the panegyric. Claudius' will was suppressed, because it might have led to unfavourable comment, preferring as it did a stepson to a son. Claudius was voted divine honours. "Yes", Nero used to remark, "mushrooms are the food of the gods."

Narcissus was killed shortly afterwards, falling, by poetic justice, hard by Messalina's tomb. Nothing in his life became him like the leaving it. Having been Claudius' private secretary, he had in his possession letters which would have incriminated Agrippina and others. He burned them all before dying.

Agrippina was now at her apogee of power. Nero was seventeen; still, she hoped, malleable. Seneca wrote admirable speeches for him; he seemed destined to become a really popular ruler. Agrippina took charge of affairs. Nero, asked by the picket for the watchword, gave 'The best of Mothers'. She attended meetings of the Senate, adopting a method of eavesdropping: she listened to the proceedings unseen from behind a door over which a curtain had been hung. Queen Victoria used almost the same device when after the death of the Prince Consort she could not bear to meet her Privy Council. She sat in an adjoining room, and murmured her agreement through the open door. Only in this respect can Queen Victoria be held to have resembled Agrippina.

The proud empress went further. She would receive embassies.

Once when an Armenian delegation were stating their case before
Nero, Agrippina appeared. She was just about to mount the
dais and sit beside her son. Everyone was appalled. Seneca
intervened just in time. He told Nero to go down and meet his
mother. He did so, and then led her aside as though to seek her
counsel privately. Seneca and Burrus now assumed control of
affairs, leaving Nero to his own unsavoury devices. Agrippina
realised that he was drifting away from her, that when it came to
a choice between filial obedience and obedience to his lusts,
Nero would always choose the latter. For instance, one day
Nero had ordered ten million sesterces to be given to one of his
catamites, Doryphorus by name, who was also his secretary for
petitions. Agrippina had the money piled up in a heap, hoping
that when he saw it Nero would change his mind. He did.
"I didn't realise I'd been so mean," he said, "double it." On
another occasion he was going through the imperial wardrobe,
which had belonged to, and been augmented by, former empresses. Picking out a magnificent cloak, encrusted with jewels,
he sent it to his mother, knowing full well how she loved to
dazzle those who beheld her. On receiving it Agrippina merely
observed that in sending her but one paltry garment he was
swindling her out of her rightful property.

Clearly a crisis was impending. Nero hit back by expelling
Pallas, his mother's paramour, from the palace. (He was not
killed until seven years later.)

Agrippina was alarmed, Nero nervous. The breach widened.
The empress lost her self-control. She foolishly allowed her
indignation to become vocal. She let Nero hear her say that
Britannicus was now grown up, and that he was the true son and
heir of his father, and that the empire rightfully belonged to him,
and not to an adopted usurper who took advantage of it to bully
his mother. Unflinchingly, she reviewed the sins of the doomed
imperial family, without sparing her own marriage or the murder
of her husband. "But thank heaven", she said, "my stepson is
still alive. I will take him to the barracks. Let the Guard hear
me, the daughter of Germanicus, pitted against the men who
claim to rule the whole world—Burrus with his withered hand,
and Seneca the deportee with the professional voice." She
gesticulated, she raved, she railed, invoking the deified Claudius,
the spirits of the Silani, and all her own unavailing crimes.

Nero was deeply perturbed. He knew his mother well enough

to be sure that she was not talking idly—she really might contrive that Britannicus should be preferred to him. Shortly before Britannicus' fourteenth birthday, when according to Roman custom, he would officially achieve manhood, the Saturnalia were celebrated. At this season, corresponding roughly to our Christmas and New Year festivities, restraints were cast aside, even by slaves, and everyone made merry. Nero and his intimates were playing a game, at which dice were cast to elect a 'king', who then ordered the rest to perform various antics. Thinking to make Britannicus a figure of fun, Nero, who was of course the 'king', bade him stand in the middle and sing a song. Britannicus, with complete assurance, because his voice was better than Nero's, sang a pathetic ballad about a youth who was wrongly deprived of his home and heritage—meaning himself. The rest of the company were visibly affected. Nero made up his mind to kill Britannicus. He could not do it openly, because Britannicus could not be charged with any misdemeanour. He decided to contrive it secretly. Already Britannicus was surrounded by unscrupulous and disloyal servants. Locusta was again called in. Her first concoction was too weak, and only acted as an aperient. Locusta was summoned and Nero assailed her with his own hands. Her excuse was that she did not wish Nero to be saddled with so heinous a crime. "D'you think I'm afraid of the Julian law against assassination?" he said. Then and there in a room of the palace, she was told to mix the strongest brew she could. It was tried on a kid, but the animal lingered for five hours. The mixture was fortified again and again, so that when finally it was given to a pig, the beast instantly fell dead. All was now ready.

At dinner, Britannicus sat not at the high table, but, as is still the custom in some noble Italian families, at a separate table in the same room, with his coevals. There could thus be no question of any physical contact between him and Nero. Britannicus had a 'taster' who duly handed him a hot drink. This was harmless, but too hot for Britannicus. Cold water, containing the poison, was added to it. Britannicus drank of it and instantly fell to the ground. After a brief muscular convulsion he ceased to breathe. Nero affected to take no notice. "He's always been epileptic," he said and went on with the feast. Agrippina was horrified: if Nero could murder his brother, how long would his mother be safe?

Britannicus' corpse was hurried away to an already prepared pyre, and his ashes were placed in the family mausoleum. Nero had smeared the face with gypsum, to hide the livid patches caused by the poison. But a shower of rain washed the gypsum off, so that as the body was being carried through the Forum people not only heard rumours of the crime but saw the evidence of it with their own eyes. Tacitus adds that it was generally believed that Nero had defiled his brother for some time previously so that "his death might have seemed to come none too soon, and to be the lesser outrage". Locusta was lavishly rewarded, and her previous crimes forgotten.

Agrippina now understood just how vulnerable she was. Nero had withdrawn her bodyguard and guard of honour. He had turned her out of the palace and installed her in one of the family's dower houses. It was immediately deserted. Nero himself only paid fleeting visits now and then, always attended by an armed guard. He was always encouraging her to take country holidays. "Her only visitors and comforters were a few women who called because they loved her—or hated her." One of these was Silana, widow of the unfortunate Gaius Silius, Messalina's victim. Aggripina had prevented Silana from marrying again, saying she was old and vicious. Agrippina did not want the prospective husband for herself: she wanted Silana's wealth. Silana put up two of her dependants to prosecute Agrippina, on the ground that she was forming a party to unseat Nero, and replace him by a man who possessed the same relationship to the divine Augustus as he did, whose empress Agrippina was to be. The plot leaked out before the prosecution was actually undertaken. Nero was so frightened that he wanted to murder his mother at once. Burrus restrained him, pointing out that all they had to go on so far was the story of one man—mere hearsay. Everyone was entitled to an opportunity for defence, especially a parent.

Next day, Burrus called on Agrippina, to inform her of the accusation. She must either refute it or pay the penalty. Seneca and certain ex-slaves were there. Agrippina put on one of her best performances. That old hag Silana! She was childless; how could she understand a mother's feelings? As for Domitia, Nero's aunt and Agrippina's deadly enemy, all she did was to concoct melodramas with her lover Atimetus (the man who had divulged the so-called plot), and amuse herself in improving

a) Titus

b) Domitian

c) Nerva

a) Empress Plotina, the wife of Trajan, a bust in the
Vatican Museum

b) Trajan

c) Plotina

her fishponds at Baiae. Agrippina's listeners were touched, and
tried to calm her. She demanded to see Nero. When he appeared,
she made no defence. Instead, she secured rewards for her sup-
porters, and revenge on her accusers. Silana was exiled, her two
would-be prosecutors expelled, Atimetus executed.

Racine makes of this confrontation of mother and son (though
he displaces it in time, making it take place before, not after
Britannicus' murder) one of the greatest scenes in European
drama. Agrippina pronounces her apologia in a masterpiece of no
less than 112 uninterrupted lines, more than twice the length
of Shakespeare's longest. Nero remains unmoved. The final line
of the play is one of perfect irony. Agrippina says to Burrus that
she trusts her son's 'remorse' will lead him into better ways, to
which Burrus replies, "May the gods grant that this be his last
crime." As all Racine's audiences knew, it was to be only his
first. (See Appendix I.)

Coinage is one of the best political barometers we possess for
Roman affairs. At the beginning of Nero's reign we find him and
his mother happily facing each other on the obverse of the coinage.
Then Agrippina is relegated to the reverse, and finally she dis-
appears from the imperial coins altogether. That was what she
must now do in reality, Nero decided. The dénouement
was caused by a woman, Poppaea Sabina, daughter of the Poppaea whose end Messalina had encompassed. Nero had heard
of her charms from her husband Otho, a younger member of
Nero's circle. He was constantly praising her beauty. Nero
demanded to see her. When he did so, he fell madly in love.
He was determined to have her. He had long been bored by his
wife Octavia. When his friends upbraided him, he replied with
a brutal jest: she ought, he said, to be satisfied with the insignia
of wifehood; just as men might be awarded consular or triumphal
insignia without having held office or fought battles, so Octavia
should be content with being the emperor's wife in name only.

The one stumbling-block now remaining was Agrippina.
Seneca suborned Acte, Nero's mistress, to tell Nero that everyone
was talking about the improper relations between him and his
mother, that she was boasting about it, and that the troops would
not tolerate that sort of emperor. Nero was thenceforth at pains
never to be alone with her. But he soon realised that her death
was the one and only solution to his marital problems. So long
as she lived, he dare not divorce Octavia, in favour of Poppaea.

F

But how could he encompass her end? To stage a third dinner-death would be too incriminating. Poison had no effect on Agrippina, who had for long been taking immunising antidotes. A direct assassination would be far too risky. Besides, it might fail.

An ex-slave called Anicetus, who had formerly been Nero's tutor, was now in command of the fleet at Misenum. He and the empress hated each other. He now put forward a plan which captivated Nero by its novel theatricality. There had recently appeared on the stage a ship which automatically parted asunder, let out some beasts and then came together again so as to be once more seaworthy. That would be just the thing. So a ship of the same kind was constructed. Nero, bent on Agrippina's death, now fauned upon her. It was March in the year 59. Nero decided that, as was his wont, he would attend the feast of Minerva at Baiae. He took his mother with him, in a galley which was furnished with every refinement of luxury. They disembarked at Antium (Anzio), Nero's birthplace. Nero went on to Baiae. A few days later he invited his mother to dinner. She came by sea as far as Bauli, a pretty little villa between Misenum and Baiae. Her vessel was rammed, seemingly by accident, so as to make it unseaworthy; but other ships were standing there. "One," says Tacitus, "more sumptuous than the rest was evidently another compliment to his mother, who had formerly been accustomed to travel in warships manned by the imperial navy." Nero greeted his mother with affectionate fervour. But perhaps she had some foreboding. According to Suetonius, Nero had already tried to kill her by arranging that the panels of her bedroom ceiling should fall on her as she slept. That plot miscarried, but it must have put her on the alert. Someone, it is said, now warned her to be on her guard against a new attempt. Agrippina could not decide whether or not to believe the story, but to be on the safe side made the journey from Bauli to Baiae in a sedan-chair.

Her fears were allayed by Nero's reception of her. The party was a great success and went on far into the night. When his mother left, Nero saw her off, in the beautiful new ship, her own being by her son's contrivance no longer serviceable. His parting caresses were more tender than ever. The rest of the night he passed in intense anxiety. The ship set sail. The sea was calm, the stars were shining. At a given signal, the roof of the cabin, loaded with lead, duly collapsed. It killed one of Agrippina's male attendants, but she and her waiting-woman Acceronia

were saved by the raised sides of her couch, which arrested the
fall of the weighted ceiling. General confusion followed, those
who were in the plot trying to capsize the ship, those who were
not, trying to keep it on an even keel. The ladies perforce took
to the water. Acceronia bravely tried to save her mistress by
calling out that she was Agrippina, and imploring help. She
was soon despatched by blows from oars and spars. Agrippina,
despite a wound on the shoulder, simply swam to some fishing-
boats, which landed her safely at the Lucrine lake, from which
she was taken home.

That this had happened so close to the shore, on a windless
night, the vessel unscathed by any rock, convinced Agrippina that
it was a murderous attempt. Her only hope was to pretend she
thought it was an accident. So she wrote to Nero saying that she
had been saved from death, only slightly wounded, by divine
mercy and his lucky star. All she now needed was rest. Naturally
the incident aroused the whole neighbourhood, and people
rushed to the shore with lights, and waded into the sea to find
out what had occurred. Nero was appalled. Anything might
happen. He sent for Seneca and Burrus, who were asleep near by.
Seneca asked Burrus whether the troops could be relied upon to
do what Anicetus had failed to accomplish. No, said Burrus,
the soldiers were loyal to the imperial house and to Germanicus'
memory. Then Agrippina's messenger arrived. While he was
handing over the letter, Nero dropped a sword at his feet: he
would pretend that Agrippina had sent the man to kill him. The
innocent messenger was at once arrested. His mother must now
be killed without delay, so that Nero could represent her death
as a guilty suicide. Anicetus undertook to succeed on land when
he had failed by sea. Off he went with a squad of marines. He
surrounded Agrippina's house, and forced an entry. Agrippina,
deserted even by her maid, knew that her end had come. "If you
have come to visit me," she said to Anicetus, "you can report
that I am better. If you are murderers, I know my son is not
responsible. My son did not order his mother's death." The
killers closed in. One hit her on the head with a truncheon.
Then as Anicetus' lieutenant drew his sword, "Strike here,"
she said, pointing to her womb, "this bore Nero." Blow followed
blow until she was dead. (An Eton master of fifty years ago is
reported to have commented, "I don't think an English lady
would have said that.")

Nero retired to Naples, whence he wrote a long letter to the Senate, denouncing his mother. Her death, he said, was a national blessing, and as a national blessing the servile Senate celebrated it.

Of all the wives of the Caesars, Agrippina excites the most compassion. She was born into a vile world. She did vile things. She was cruel and she was fatally ambitious, both for herself and her son. We do not know what she confided to her memoirs, now lost. But she had expected her death for years. When she had asked the astrologers about Nero, they had told her that he would become emperor but would kill his mother. "Let him kill me," she had replied, "so long as he becomes emperor."

Agrippina's corpse was cremated and buried in a modest grave by the road that led to Misenum "on the heights where Julius Caesar's mansion overlooks the bay below".

★   ★   ★

Whatever we may think of Agrippina and of her fate, her memory is fragrant to this day. She had been born when her parents were stationed on the Rhine, at the capital of a friendly tribe called the Ubii. To commemorate her birthplace, Nero had established a Roman military settlement there. It was called Colonia Agrippinensis in honour of the empress. When, in 1709, Johann Maria Farina started his business in the city, he called his product 'Eau de Cologne'.

CHAPTER VI

The End of the Line

AT THE BEGINNING of his *Histories*, written in or about AD
115, Tacitus recites the horrors of the Neronian and post-
Neronian age, at home and abroad, and then inserts this remarkable passage:

> And yet the age was not so barren of all virtue as not to exhibit
> some noble examples. Mothers followed their sons, wives their
> husbands, into exile; some kinsmen showed courage, some
> sons-in-law were faithful; there were slaves who held out
> staunchly even against torture, and illustrious men who bore
> their doom with fortitude; there were death-scenes as noble
> as those celebrated by antiquity.
> And in addition to these manifold disasters in human affairs,
> there were prodigies in earth and sky; there were warnings
> from lightning, there were presages for the future, some of
> good, some of evil, some obscure, some not to be misunder-
> stood: for never did the people of Rome endure calamities
> more grievous, never witness more convincing proof that the
> Gods care much for our chastisement, for our happiness not
> at all.

This passage is of prime importance in understanding the epoch
we have now reached. Tacitus was a boy at the time he describes
(he was born in AD 55), but looking back over half a century, he
fully realised its ominous significance, which in broad terms was
that virtue and honour were rare, exceptions to the general run
of affairs, which was evil, and secondly that the age was one of

intense pessimism. The gods were there to punish, not to save, nor even to guide. Like every Roman, Tacitus—a man of excellent understanding—was lapped in superstition: omens and prodigies furnished the guidance which neither faith nor reason were able to supply. Men lived without hope, and many saw in death a release from suffering. The mere idea that hope should be a major virtue, as St Paul, who reached Rome in the year 61, had proclaimed it to be, would be quite beyond the grasp of the ordinary Roman. Even Stoicism, which many of the best spirits of the day embraced, even that was a chilly creed. Like all puritan codes, it contrived to make the second-best of both worlds. Its best-known exponent in those days was Seneca himself. But what Seneca preached and what Seneca practised were two very different things. He had encouraged Nero in his excesses, he was privy to the murder of Agrippina, and he had amassed an enormous fortune. Nero drove him to suicide. Murder, the taking of another's life, was now a commonplace; and if murder, why not suicide?

It was against this sombre background that the drama of Nero's latter days was to be played out; and it was a woman who provoked it. As de Montherlant puts it, in *Pitié pour les femmes*, "*Les pires ennemies des femmes sont les femmes.*" By far the most interesting of the women now at war, was Poppaea. The other two antagonists were Acte and Octavia. Seneca and his associates encouraged Nero's lust for Acte: after all, she was an underling, and it was better for everyone that Nero should be infatuated with her rather than with ladies of consequence, with whom a liaison might produce complications both personal and political. Besides, she had been a useful tool in the plot which made an end of Agrippina. Let her be: she kept Nero out of mischief, which to them meant that they, and not he, would rule the state.

Poppaea did not see it in that light at all, nor did Nero. To Nero marriage was little more than a charade. His union with Sporus was balanced by another, in which Nero took the role of the wife, the husband being a freedman called Pythagoras. "The emperor, in the presence of witnesses, put on the bridal veil. Dowry, marriage bed, wedding torches, all were there. Indeed everything was public which even in a natural union is veiled by night." (Both these unions were celebrated, later on, in Greece; but Nero's carefree lewdness was ingrained in him long before.)

His passion for Poppaea was something altogether different. He really was in love with her, ardently and unswervingly. Poppaea, despite the awful background she knew so well, the intrigues and killings which had plagued her kith and kin, her first marriage to the very man who had driven her mother to suicide, and had then been ruined by Agrippina, despite her present marriage to Otho, one of Nero's intimates—despite all, Poppaea was determined to become empress. Otho was fatally faithful to her. As for Poppaea herself, here is Tacitus' picture, one of his best.

Poppaea had every asset except goodness. From her mother, the loveliest woman of her day, she inherited distinction and beauty. Her wealth, too, was equal to her birth. She was clever, and pleasant to talk to. She seemed respectable. But her life was depraved. Her public appearances were few; she would half-veil her face at them, to stimulate curiosity (or because it suited her). To her, married or bachelor bedfellows were alike. She was indifferent to her reputation—yet insensible to men's love, and herself unloving. Advantage dictated the bestowal of her favours.

While married to a knight called Rufrius Crispus (p. 62)—to whom she had borne a son—she was seduced by Marcus Salvius Otho, an extravagant youth who was regarded as peculiarly close to Nero. Their liaison was quickly converted into marriage. Otho praised her charms and graces to the emperor. This was either a lover's indiscretion, or a deliberate stimulus prompted by the idea that joint possession of Poppaea would be a bond reinforcing Otho's own power. As he left the emperor's table, he was often heard saying he was going to his wife, who had brought him what all men want and only the fortunate enjoy, nobility and beauty.

Under such provocations, delay was brief. Poppaea obtained access to Nero, and established her ascendancy. First she used flirtacious wiles, pretending to be unable to resist her passion for Nero's looks. Then, as the emperor fell in love with her, she became haughty, and if he kept her for more than two nights, she insisted she was married and could not give up her marriage. "I am devoted to Otho. My relations with him are unique. His character and way of living are both fine. *There* is a man for whom nothing is too good. Whereas you,

Nero, are kept down because the mistress you live with is a servant, Acte. What a sordid, dreary, menial association!"

Could Flaubert have done it better?

But Poppaea was more than just an *intriguante*. She took herself seriously, both in body and spirit. She was now, in the year 58, twenty-seven to Nero's twenty-one. Her auburn hair was dressed in a new fashion, with her tresses massed in a glittering sheaf— the fashion which was to endure, farcically elaborated, into the next century. Five hundred wild asses provided her bath-milk. When she went abroad, the mules which drew her carriage pranced on gilded hooves. The scents she used were called Poppaean, long after her death.

Poppaea's spiritual experiences have an interest which transcends her carnal failings. Nero, so Suetonius tells us, and we can well believe him, despised all religious cults, except that of the Syrian goddess, Atargatis, and even her influence was so transitory that he once made water on her image. Poppaea, on the other hand, admired Judaism, and became a member of that fringe group, who, without joining the Jewish community, adopted much of their belief and practice. That Poppaea should have done so, is evidence of the number and status which the Mosaic cult had attained in Rome. When Josephus, the Jewish historian, came to Italy in AD 64, to pleaed the cause of some of his compatriots who had been sent under arrest to Rome, he asked a Jewish court actor called Aliturus, to secure for him an audience with Poppaea. He duly met her at Puteoli. And his countrymen, priests, were released at her behest. There is no evidence that Poppaea induced Nero to make scapegoats of the Christians after the disastrous fire in that year. That they were so abused and for the first time brutally persecuted is, nevertheless, testimony to the fact that only three years after the coming of St Paul to Rome they were recognised as a separate community.

Poppaea has thus the distinction of being the first empress to investigate, even to patronise and protect, the Jewish faith, from which was to emerge the very religion which has made Rome its hearth and home. Even Acte comes within the moralist's purview. She had it seems a Christian freedman. She may even have been a convert herself: as we know from St Paul's letter to the Philippians (v, 22), there were adherents of the new religion in the service of the emperor.

For Poppaea, religion was a pastime: what she was out for was less salvation in another world than power in this. She had started nagging Nero even before Agrippina's death.

"He was an emperor under orders", she said—master neither of the empire nor of himself. "Otherwise why these postponements of our marriage? I suppose my looks and victorious ancestors are not good enough. Or do you distrust my capacity to bear children? Or the sincerity of my love? No! I think you are afraid that, if we were married, I might tell you frankly how the Senate is downtrodden and the public enraged by your mother's arrogance and greed. If Agrippina can only tolerate daughters-in-law who hate her son, let me be Otho's wife again. I will go anywhere in the world where I only need hear of the emperor's humiliations, rather than see them—and see you in danger like myself." This appeal was reinforced by tears and all a lover's tricks.

Nero was won, and so Agrippina met her end. But still, three years later, Nero had not married Poppaea. True, there had been external affairs to worry about. The Britons had risen in revolt. Seneca had lent them forty million sesterces, and now demanded it back. Boadicea had been on the rampage. Colchester and St Alban's had been sacked. The less important commercial centre of London was pillaged. It had taken a full-scale campaign to quell the islanders.

Boadicea poisoned herself. The general who had taken over the command in Britain, "neither provoking the enemy, nor himself provoked called this ignoble inactivity peace with honour".

Meanwhile in Rome the situation of the country was deteriorating every day. Burrus was dead, poisoned by Nero, it was said. He was succeeded as commander of the praetorians by a vile low-born Sicilian called Tigellinus, who had already once been banished but had returned to be Prefect of the City and was now commander of the Guards. Burrus' death undermined the position of Seneca, his colleague and accomplice for so long. It was only because they had the Guard at their backs that they had been able to do what they did, be it good or bad. Seneca knew that the promotion of Tigellinus was an implicit invitation to retire. This he now did, after an emotional interview with Nero, whose guide, philosopher and friend he had been, he said, for fourteen years. He was to survive for three more, and to fall a victim to his master in 65, for his alleged complicity in a conspiracy to unseat Nero.

Most Romans were by now tired of him. As the historian Merivale so aptly put it: "In his stilted truisms or transparent paradoxes Seneca represents an age of overweening presumption and pretence." The philosophising millionaire was himself a paradox. His high moral tone when he was in the pulpit was un-questioned, except by those who knew how he behaved in between sermons. These were, naturally enough, in the minority; and for many a century Seneca remained the paragon of virtue, simply on the strength of his writings. He was lauded by Dante, he appears in the *Roman de la Rose* in the thirteenth century, and in the *Golden Legend* of Iacobo de Voragine, which Caxton printed in 1483. Seneca indeed has influenced the manners of our own day. Besides his moral works, he wrote a number of plays. These were intended not for the vulgar stage, but to be recited in the salons of Rome. They were packed with 'points' some of which were very effective. When in the sixteenth century, drama was revived, it was to Seneca that the rising dramatists turned, as for instance in *Gorboduc*, the first historical English tragedy, produced by Sackville and Norton in 1561. Seneca's influence on classical French drama in the next century is even more marked. In our own day, Seneca can be claimed as the original from which our radio drama has ultimately developed.

Nero felt that, with the removal of Burrus and the relegation of Seneca, he could give full rein to his own desires. Prominent men were killed without trial, one simply because he was descended from Augustus. Now at last he could get rid of Octavia. And happily enough in that very year 62, Poppaea was pregnant. So Nero decided to marry her, after eliminating Octavia. Octavia was unassuming, but for that reason she was popular with the citizenry, which was in itself enough to make Nero hate her. Poppaea first of all incited one of Octavia's household to accuse Octavia of adultery with a slave—an Alexandrian flute-player called Eucaerus. Her slaves were tortured. One of them, called Pythias, refused to incriminate her mistress. Tigellinus was conducting the torture. Pythias spat in his face and said: "My mistress's private parts are cleaner than your mouth, Tigellinus."

The charge of adultery was dropped: Octavia was merely

divorced. Twelve days later Nero married Poppaea: she was empress at last. But still she pursued Octavia with all her determined hatred. Octavia knew she was doomed—there had been attempts to strangle her even while she was still titular empress. The populace showed clearly enough its affection for Octavia and its hatred of Poppaea. There were riots; a mob broke into the palace. Nero is reported to have wished to take Octavia back. So frightened was he by the demonstrations. In his extremity he turned once more to Anicetus, who had killed Agrippina. He thought out a typically Neronian scheme. The mere sight of Anicetus was a perpetual reminder of his worst crime. Why not put Anicetus out of sight, and so out of mind, and at the same time kill off Octavia? Anicetus was summoned. All he had to do was to make a declaration that Octavia was his mistress. Anicetus knew that refusal would mean death. He publicly admitted that he was Octavia's lover. He went further: Octavia's object in forming this liaison was, the testified, the undermining of the loyalty of the fleet at Misenum, which Anicetus commanded, so as to incite it to rebellion. Anicetus was 'banished' to Sardinia, where he came to a remarkable end: he died a natural death.

Poor Octavia. The Romans hung garlands on her statues, and overturned those of Poppaea. On her divorce, she had been given the ominous gift of Burrus' former house and that of Rebellius Plautus, the man whose crime it was to have been a descendant of Augustus. But now she was hustled away to the island of Pandateria under armed guard. Poppaea had as usual been arrogant and cringing by turns. Either mood worked on Nero, crazed as he was with suspicion. She fell at Nero's feet crying: "Now that things have reached this pass, it is not marriage I am fighting for, but what to me means less than my marriage—my life. It is in danger from Octavia's dependants and slaves. They commit in peace-time outrages that could hardly happen in war! The emperor is their target—they only lack a leader. And once disorders begin one will easily be found when she leaves Campania and proceeds to the capital. Even her distant nod causes riots.

"What have *I* done wrong? Whom have I injured? Or is this all because I am going to give an authentic heir to the house of the Caesars? Would Rome prefer an Egyptian flute-player's child to be introduced into the Palace? If you think it best, take back your directress voluntarily. Or else safeguard yourself. Punish suitably. No secrecy was needed to end the first troubles.

Besides, once they lose hope of Nero keeping Octavia, they will find her another husband.''

As Tacitus says, Octavia had virtually died on her wedding-day. Her new home had brought her nothing but misery. Her father Claudius had been murdered, so had her brother Britannicus. A maid, Acte, had been preferred to her mistress. Now she knew, after this foul and forged imputation of unchastity, that it was her turn to die. The executioners arrived on the island two days after her. ''She was hardly a living person any more, so certain was she of imminent destruction. Yet she lacked the peace of death. She protested that she was a wife no longer, only Nero's sister. She invoked the memory of her ancestors, she even invoked Agrippina, in whose days her marriage had been unhappy certainly, but not fatal.'' All to no avail. Octavia was trussed up, and then bled to death—or almost. Her terror retarded the flow of blood, so she was put into an exceedingly hot vapour bath, and suffocated. Her head was cut off, and sent to Rome for Poppaea to gloat over. If ever there was the wife of a Caesar who was above suspicion, it was Octavia; and that is how she died, in her twentieth year.

On 21st January 63, Poppaea gave birth to a daughter at Antium, Nero's own birthplace. She was called Claudia, but soon she was elevated, like her mother, to the rank of Augusta. A temple was decreed to the goddess Fecundity. In less than four months the child was dead. She was at once declared a goddess, and voted a place on the gods' ceremonial couch, with a shrine and a priest. Just what did 'deification' really imply? It must be borne in mind, that to a Roman, *a* god was in no sense like *the* God of the Judaeo-Christian ethic. Many Romans laughed at the whole idea of making a human being into a divinity. Seneca had ridiculed the notion in his skit on Claudius' deification: *pumkinification* he called it. Vespasian would joke about it as he neared death; ''I think I'm becoming a god,'' he said. Serious minds like Pausanias and Plutarch flouted it. Julian the Apostate was to call Augustus a 'doll-maker' for countenancing it. It was little more than a posthumous honour, a sort of honorary sancti-fication. The best modern analogue to it would be the phrase 'His Most Sacred Majesty' as applied to the Hanoverian monarchs of Britain. Nobody would really account King William IV as most sacred; but it looked the thing on the invitations to his coronation.

Two years later, in 65, Poppaea was expecting a second child. Nero had spent the day at the races, in which he had competed. He was tired and irritable. Poppaea took him to task for being so late. Nero kicked her. She died of a miscarriage. Her corpse was embalmed like that of an oriental sovereign and placed in the family mausoleum. Nero now had no heir. He must marry again. But to be on the safe side, he thought it only prudent to kill Poppaea's child by her first marriage. He was a mere boy: Nero ordered him to be drowned by the child's own slaves, while fishing, because he used (it was said) to play at being a general and an emperor. Nero now apparently proposed marriage to his surviving half-sister, and put her to death when she refused. Poppaea was duly deified. He did nevertheless find another bride. He picked a former mistress, a rich and cultivated woman called Statilia Messalina. Statilia's attitude to marriage really did represent what Samuel Johnson would one day call the triumph of hope over experience. She had been married four times before, her current husband who was a consul at the time, being forced to commit suicide. Statilia prefigured Katherine Parr. She behaved so prudently that she survived Nero. She did not apparently go to Greece with Nero on his celebrated triumphal tour in 66, the official consort for that jaunt being Sporus, who reminded Nero of Poppaea, he said.

Nero met his end, in timorous squalor, in 68. Rome had cast him out at last, so he made his way disguised to a villa of one of his freedmen, accompanied by Sporus and three others. He was recognised, after vainly trying to kill Sporus, who ran away. When he heard the soldiers approaching he killed himself. Acte saw to his burial: she had been his first mistress and she alone was faithful to him, even after death.

Like Agrippina, both Octavia and Poppaea were to achieve posthumous immortality. Octavia became the subject of a tragedy which survives. *Octavia* it is called, and is usually to be found included in the works of Seneca, who was for long regarded as its author. It cannot be Seneca's work. Not only is he one of the actors in it, but the play shows knowledge of the circumstances of Nero's death, which took place three years after Seneca's. The style is Seneca's, and it may well have been the work of one of his pupils. It takes its colour from Greek drama. It has moving passages in it, but is read now only by those who are interested in the rare and bizarre. In death as in life Octavia was timid and retiring.

Not so Poppaea. She had once looked at herself in a mirror, and had begged the gods not to let her live when she had ceased to be attractive. That wish at least was granted to her. She was only thirty-five, if that, when she was killed. She was duly 'deified'; but another and more abiding immortality was to be hers. She is the protagonist of Monteverdi's master-work *L'Incoronazione di Poppaea*, which appeared in 1642. Monteverdi was already famous for his madrigals, of which the eighth book had been published in 1638, when he was seventy-five. He had been born in Cremona, but in 1613 he had been appointed *maestro di capella* at St Mark's Venice, a post he held until his death in 1643. Up to 1637, music had been the monopoly of the rich and powerful; but in that year the first public opera-house was opened in Venice. Monteverdi at once saw what a splendid field this opened for his genius. He composed several operas, all on mythological themes, the latest being *Il Ritorno d'Ulisse in Patria*; but he realised, as Racine was to do after him, that historical persons and events had a far more immediate appeal for an audience, especially a general audience, who were not just the *habitués* of a court salon. Like Verdi two centuries later, Monteverdi had reserved the greatest of his creations until old age—the year before his death in fact. *L'Incoronazione*, amazingly enough, is the work of an innovator, with its union of tragedy, comedy and pathos. That it is the wicked who win, would not have repelled a Venetian audience of the seventeenth century, for whom characterisation was far more important than character. The Farewell of Seneca is magnificent, dignified and resigned. Even comedy is introduced when Nero is seen revelling with his intimates. The opera is beyond question the greatest production in Italian drama of the seventeenth century. It is only comparatively recently that it has attained universal renown. And with it Poppaea has triumphed for all time.

From the Palatine to Glyndebourne might seem a long and fanciful journey. But not for Poppaea: it seems quite natural that Poppaea should have set her heart on the highest, and should have achieved it.

Part II

CHAPTER VII

The Flavians

NO ERA EVER thinks it will come to an end; but they all do.

From the victory of Octavian (Augustus) over Antony and Cleopatra at Actium in 31 BC until the death of Nero in AD 68, the Julio-Claudian family had ruled Rome. It had been a century of glory and—outside the Palace—of tranquillity seldom equalled in history. The 'eternity' which Romans ascribed to their city and its dominions—Vespasian was to put the magic word on his coinage—was no empty boast.

Now the dynasty who had created it was defunct. In some ways that was a blessing. Of the five members of the family who had ruled from the Palatine, only Augustus, aided by Livia, could be accounted a success throughout his length of days. Tiberius died unloved, Gaius was murdered, Claudius was an industrious buffoon, Nero a calamity. Ten years after Nero's death there was only one survivor of the Julian line, Junia Calvina. She was a granddaughter of the younger Julia, and possessed much of her gaiety. She had been banished by Agrippina but brought back by Nero. (Banishment under the Julio-Claudians was almost as much part of the protocol for smart ladies as 'presentation' was to be under a more recent régime.) Junia outlived the whole dynasty and lived on until the days of Vespasian. When, as he lay on his death-bed in 79, it was reported to him that the doors of the imperial mausoleum had opened of their own accord, as Roman holy doors not infrequently did, he remarked, "To make way for Junia Calvina, no doubt." Strange as it may seem, not even Nero died wholly unregretted. Our accounts of him were written when other dynasties ruled Rome, and it was therefore tactful, and perhaps prophylactic, to play down the last of the Julio-Claudians. Vitellius paid him public honours, which included readings of poems from *The Book of the Master* (Nero), Suetonius writing early in the second century concludes his life of Nero with the following remarkable paragraph:

> There were some who for a long time decorated his tomb with spring and summer flowers and now produced his statues on the Rostra with the fringed toga, and now his edicts, as if he were still alive and would shortly return and deal destruction to his enemies. Nay more, Vologaesus king of the Parthians, when he sent envoys to the Senate to renew his alliance, earnestly begged this too, that honour be paid to the memory of Nero. In fact twenty years later when I was a young man, a person of obscure origin appeared who gave out that he was Nero, and the name was still so much in favour with the Parthians that they supported him vigorously and surrendered him with much reluctance.

That was in 88: a first pseudo-Nero had appeared in 69, a second ten years later. Nero was only thirty-two when he died and there is no doubt that this theatrical blue-eyed blond did appeal to the emotional orient, rather than to chilly Roman hearts; but that does not alter the political truth, as summed up by Tacitus:

> The death of Nero was at first greeted with transports of delight; but it gave rise to many reflections not only in the city—in the minds of the Fathers, the populace and the garrison—but also among the legions and their generals, for now the secret of the Empire had been divulged, that emperors could be made elsewhere than in Rome.

The whole Empire, from Spain to Syria, was to be involved in the ensuing chaos. In the spring of 68, the insurrection of Vindex in Gaul encouraged the army in Spain to hail as imperator Galba, their commander, a well-born but stingy martinet, who in reply to the demands of his troops for larger bribes, said that he was accustomed to enrol troops, not to buy them—a remark which branded him as an anachronism. At the age of seventy-six, he marched on Rome, to be hailed as emperor. He showed himself, in Tacitus' phrase, "by general consent just the man to be emperor—if only he hadn't been". He was tolerated for seven months, and then butchered in the Forum itself on 15th January 69, and his head carried to the next player in this ghastly game of Roman roulette, namely Otho, who was still in his thirties, the bewigged and scented fop who had been Poppaea's first husband. He had hoped that, in supporting Galba, he was backing a winner, and that the old man would adopt him as his successor. When Galba adopted someone else, Otho became his enemy. Poor Otho, a 'transient and embarrassed phantom' if ever there was one. During his brief tenure of the purple, he had little time to do more than restore Poppaea's statues, which had been overthrown by the mob in 62, when they were showing their indignation at the death of Octavia; but they had been restored, and were probably again cast down after Nero's death.

Otho lasted but three months. A third competitor was now in the field, Vitellius, who commanded the army of the Rhine, having been sent there (nobody knew why) by Galba. Otho tried to temporise with him, in vain. Vitellius, a notorious glutton, guzzled his way southward. One corps of his army defeated Otho's forces near Cremona, whereupon Otho killed himself; and Vitellius reached Rome.

Of all the women who took part in the dynastic puppetry of the pre-Flavian age, only one excites our pity, and that is Galeria Fundana, daughter of a praetor and second wife of Vitellius. His first wife Petronilla had given him a son who was one-eyed. Vitellius murdered the boy, who was heir to a fortune, which came in very handy to the prodigal but indigent father. Petronilla was soon divorced and married off to Dolabella, a well-known senator whom Vitellius murdered as soon as he had the power to do so. Vitellius was such a spendthrift that he was forced to mortgage his house to a tax-farming syndicate, removing Fundana and his mother to a squalid apartment. His honest mother Sextilia was forced to sell her jewellery, Vitellius even plucking a valuable pearl from her ear to pay for his travelling expenses when he went north to take up the provincial appointment which Galba gave him.

Fundana, therefore, can hardly have looked forward to a happy married life. She, too, bore a son to Vitellius. The boy was so tongue-tied as to be almost dumb. Fundana herself was plain, but modest, and above reproach morally. Naturally enough she found her new existence mortifying and perilous too. After Galba's death, when Otho was master, Fundana, Sextilia and the children went in fear of their lives; but Otho, either from good nature or because they were valuable hostages, did them no harm. News of Otho's death reached Vitellius in Gaul. Fundana and her son hurried north to greet him. He placed the poor little lad—he was only six—on a tribunal and gave him the titles of Germanicus and imperator. When they arrived in Rome, Vitellius saluted Fundana as Augusta on the Capitol, and himself assumed the name Germanicus. His mother said openly that her son was called Vitellius, not Germanicus, a title to which he had not the remotest right.

Vitellius affected to make light of Nero's Golden House. Dio suggests that Fundana turned up her nose at it as well. This is a piece of gossip which does not accord with Fundana's modest character. What she may well have said is that the whole place was upside down, as it must have been during two interregnums, when it was at the unmerciful mercy of the soldiery. Tacitus, who is always to be preferred as 'best evidence', assures us that she was just the same as 'empress' as she had been before. With all her influence, she did nothing but good. She even saved the life of one Trachalus, who had been Otho's speech-writer. Vitellius lived a life of swinish extravagance. He lounged away his days in the theatre and circus. It was suggested that poor Sporus, Nero's 'wife', should be brought on to the stage in the role of a virgin being ravished, but he had suffered enough outrage already, and, to avoid this ultimate shame, committed suicide. Sextilia, too, disappeared, whether by suicide or starved to death by her son, is not clear: it may be that an astrologer had predicted that if he survived his mother, he would have a easy reign and he was taking no risks. The fourth, last and best competitor for power in the dispute for succession was Vespasian. Vespasian, aged sixty, was at this time in the Levant, conducting the campaign which was to end in the destruction of Jerusalem. He had actually sent his elder son Titus to pay homage to Galba, but learning that Galba was dead, and of the events which occurred after his death, Titus turned back. Vespasian, having decided that all was now in his favour, proceeded to Egypt, and thence set sail for Italy, taking with him a large fleet of corn-ships, without which the city would starve in ten days: he knew perfectly well that his control of the food-supply was his trump card. His able but rather sinister lieutenant Licinius Mucianus was sent ahead to prepare Rome for his advent, the task of finishing off the war being committed to Titus.

When the victorious army of Vespasian approached, Vitellius lost his nerve. He tried to abdicate; he made pathetic appeals in public, holding out his little boy, and kissing him, as if to arouse pity. Even the Vestal Virgins were enlisted as suppliants. Leading Fundana and the two children (the little boy being carried in a litter) Vitellius finally quitted the Palace and made for Fundana's house on the Aventine.

Vespasian entered Rome in the autumn of 70. Vitellius begged Vespasian's troops to spare his wife and children and brother. He then took refuge in a dog-kennel, whence after being savaged by the dogs he was hauled out and led off to an ignominious death. Vitellius' body was thrown into the Tiber. Fundana seems to have recovered what was left of it, for decent burial. His brother and son were slaughtered, but Fundana and her daughter were suffered to live on. Vespasian's kindness to her daughter was the one solace of her miserable widowhood. Perhaps Vespasian saw in Fundana some of the qualities he had loved in his own grandmother, a simple countrywoman. Her rustic grange reminded him so much of her devotion to her grandson that he would often go and muse there, forbidding any alteration to be made in the house of its furniture. When, as emperor, he presided at grandiose banquets, he rejected the costly goblets of gold or crystal that were proffered to him and always drank from a little silver mug his grandmother had given him as a present.

Thus ended this tempestuous year. From the date of Nero's death on 9th June 68, to the death of Vitellius, in December 69, was really eighteen months, but Vespasian had been hailed as imperator by the troops in Egypt on 1st July 69; and he celebrated that day as the day of his accession. He was to be one of Rome's best rulers. Tacitus, in a somewhat Sybilline phrase, says he was the only emperor whose character changed for the better. He brought order out of chaos. The civil war which had ended the old Republic had been in fact a struggle between two men, that is, between Antony and Augustus; but the contests which Vespasian quelled were warfare not between rival dynasts, but between whole armies, entire provinces. And yet he succeeded in welding each to each, and all to himself.

When Nero was a little boy his mother Agrippina, seeing that he was a lover of the liberal arts, warned him not to dabble in philosophy, because such a course would be dangerous for one who was to be a ruler. Agrippina was tough herself, and realised that the lord of Rome must be of the same fibre. Vespasian was. He had shown himself to be a capable officer, especially in Britain where he is recorded to have won thirty battles, and to have subdued the Isle of Wight. He then very wisely lay low, fearing Agrippina. He had governed Africa justly and without any untoward incident, if we except his having once been pelted with turnips at Hadrumetum. Vespasian was so far from having enriched himself that, on his return to Rome, he had to mortgage all his estates to his brother and, in order to maintain himself, he took up mule-coping. What really made him was his lack of enthusiasm for Nero as a singer. During the tour of Greece, whenever Nero was singing he either walked out or fell asleep. He was therefore banished to a little out of the way town, where he remained in apprehensive obscurity, until suddenly, when he was nearly sixty, he was sent to the Levant to extinguish the Jewish revolt. It was held that a man with such an unillustrious background, who was at the same time a good soldier, would put down the insurrection without trying to put himself up.

Nero and his counsellors had miscalculated. Once Vespasian had held Rome to ransom by his control of the Egyptian corn-fleet, it was but a step to becoming master of the mistress of the world.

As a young man Vespasian had married Flavia Domitilla, who had been the favourite of a Roman knight from Sabrata, in Africa. She was not a full citizen, but was later declared to be a freeborn woman. She bore three children to Vespasian—Titus, Domitian and Domitilla. Both mother and daughter were dead before he became emperor. Vespasian did not remarry; instead he lived happily with a concubine, Antonia Caenis, a union which had a legal status in Roman law, not unlike the morganatic unions of the later Hanoverians. Caenis was clever and discreet, She had at one time been a freedwomen and secretary to Antonia, Claudius' mother. Her memory was so retentive that once when Antonia told her to expunge a very confidential and compromising missive from her tablets, Caenis replied: "That would be use-less, Madam: I remember every word you dictate to me." Many found in Caenis (who lived almost as long as Vespasian) a useful go-between, because, by the time of his accession, Vespasian was interested more in money than in love. Caenis proved a *rusée* saleswoman of honours, places and perquisites. Vespasian naturally enough took his cut.

In Dr Balsdon's words: "As concerned the court, the Flavian period is dull, as no period before it or after it is dull: it contains not a single interesting woman." No Roman empress or princess that is. Caenis was uncharacteristically prudent for one of her origin and station. It was a queen from the Levant who was to provide the one really scintillating scandal of the age. Her unique eminence must be set against the drab background of the epoch. And that is largely due to the years that preceded it.

While those manifold paroxysms were convulsing the whole world, it is hardly surprising that amid the clash of arms, not only the laws,—as Ciceros's dictum has it—kept silence, but the ladies as well. Secondly, Galba, Otho and Vitellius were tenants of the Palace for such short periods; thirdly, by the time they became emperors, every single one from Galba to Titus, was a widower. Galba had lost his high-born Lepida while Agrippina was still alive. He resisted that lady's overtures, one reason being that he preferred the intimacy of robust males. Otho's brief brush with Poppaea has already been mentioned.

We are told that Vespasian often never knew where to turn for money. The building of the Flavian amphitheatre, or Colosseum as it is better known, must have cost him millions: and yet he provided not only a suitably well-born bridegroom for his rival Vitellius' daughter, but gave her a handsome dowry and establishment. This must be accounted an act of disinterested compassion.

Together with his son Titus, Vespasian celebrated a spectacular triumph in the year 71. His younger son Domitian, rode beside the gilded chariot on a charger. Domitian already felt jealous of his elder brother, because he considered that, having been left behind in Rome during the disturbances, even forced at one point to escape capture by donning the garb of a priest of Isis, it was he who had really engineered his father's elevation. Titus was still only thirty years of age, and already a hero, already 'the world's darling', as he was called. Domitian was still in his teens. Mucianus, nevertheless, promoted him as a cloak for his own rapacious designs.

Vespasian's rule was forthright and sensible: he might well

have taken as his motto 'peace, retrenchment and reform'. Unlike the Julio-Claudians, to whose hereditary wealth millions over the preceding century had been added by theft, booty and confiscation, Vespasian was a poor man. He has been accused of avarice, and several anecdotes went the rounds to prove the charge. He put a tax on urinals (whence the French word *Vespasienne* for a public convenience) and when Titus remonstrated with him, he handed Titus a coin acquired from this unusual source, with the words "It doesn't smell, does it?" And when a deputation informed him that they would like to erect a magnificent and costly statue of him, he held out his palm, saying, "Here's the pedestal for it." Thus, despite the growing rift between his two sons, life went peaceably on, until in the year 75, Titus provided Rome with a really thrilling scandal.

While he was in Palestine, Titus met the beautiful, able and ambitious Berenice, sister of King Herod Agrippa II. It was before them, and the procurator Festus, that Paul the apostle made his celebrated defence at Caesarea in AD 60, as recorded in *Acts* xxv. She had been thrice married, and was now living in an incestuous association with her brother. She might well have defended herself, if charged with it, that the first and famous Berenice was the sister-wife of the second Ptolemy of Egypt, in accordance with Egyptian practice. She thus became known as *philadelphos*, brother-lover, a title which was then adopted by her spouse. It is to this marriage that we owe so many cities called Philadelphia in the Levant: they commemorate not brotherly love, but sisterly incest.

Berenice and Herod were in Palestine at the time of the Jewish War, which began in 66. They both quite sincerely believed, as Herod's family had believed for a century and more, that only by arriving at a *modus vivendi* with Rome could any sort of autonomy be left to Jewry. They were both rich, and Herod, though his actual kingdom was small, had the right of appointing the Jewish High Priest, and it was he who had custody of the holy vestments. It was natural, therefore, that they should become the favourites of Titus, in whose camp, indeed, they were to dwell when their own palace in Jerusalem (it was on the bluff to the west of the Tyropoeon Valley) had been burned down. Titus was a man of prismatic charm. He sang and played beautifully, he was a brilliant horseman and archer. He was a champion shorthand-writer, and used to boast that he could be the prince of forgers if he cared to be. What more natural than that Titus should be bewitched by the charms of Berenice who, even if she was past her prime—she was in the hungry forties—still had her riches?

In 75 Berenice was in Rome, and lodged in the Palace. Caenis died in this year. She may have encouraged Titus, because her old patroness Antonia, mother of Claudius, had shown great kindness to Herod's father when he was in Rome—she would certainly have given a good account of this charming Jewish family. But Berenice reckoned without the Romans. She behaved arrogantly, and even held her own court. Quintillian tells us that he pleaded before her. She was soon made to understand that the Romans would not put up with a foreign, alien crown-princess, a new Cleopatra as she seemed to many. She was given her *congé*.

Four years later, when Titus was emperor, back she came. She was again repulsed; and so acquired a fame denied to many more intelligent, if less persistent, elderly ladies. As Suetonius puts it, "Titus at once sent her away from the city, himself unwilling, she unwilling." The Latin words are *invitus invitam*. For a Roman reader, those six syllables were triply charged. Catullus in a pretty ode describing the transformation of the hair of the original Berenice into a constellation, makes a reluctant tress exclaim: "Unwillingly my queen do I quit your head." Virgil was so taken with the line that with only one word ('shore' for 'head') altered he puts it into the mouth of Aeneas as he bids farewell to Dido. Berenice, Dido, Berenice again—every reader of Suetonius would discern the triple barb.

But that was by no means the end of Berenice, of whom ancient writers tell us no more. In the year after Racine's triumph with *Britannicus*, that is in 1670, both he and Corneille produced a *Bérénice*. Racine's is by far the better play. Voltaire called it a rose-water tragedy, which it is. Posterity has confirmed Voltaire's judgment. Compared with the 1,159 official performances of *Britannicus*, by the Comédie Française, from 1680 up to the production of 8th November 1972, *Bérénice* had scored only 419, of which the last was in June 1966. Racine declared half in jest that he had produced something out of nothing, meaning that one phrase of Suetonius. The play does have its moments, such as the final 'farewell' scene, which so impressed Mlle Sagan that she called a novel by words from its third line; but it cannot be compared with *Britannicus*. Nevertheless Berenice won in the end.

Thousands who have never heard of Racine can hum the famous minuet from Handel's opera *Berenice* (1737). Only Berenice can claim the quadruple tiara of the Bible, the Palatine, the Salle Richelieu and Covent Garden. Such are the accidents of fame.

After so brilliant an interlude, it is painful to have to chronicle, however briefly, the squalor of Domitian's marital life.

Domitian would nowadays be regarded as under-privileged rather than over-sexed. His upbringing had been miserable. Early separated by political and military exigencies from his father, overshadowed by his brilliant and fashionable brother, his elder by twelve years, and with no mother to console and direct him, he soon went astray. During the civil wars of 68–69, we was left in Rome. He felt that, as the man on the spot, though he was only a stripling, he had contributed to the ensuing triumph, and that he was underrated. When his father died, he accused Titus of having tampered with the will, which would have left him joint Caesar and heir. Titus could have done so: did he not boast of his skill at counterfeiting? On his death-bed he said he had to regret only one thing in his life. What that was, he did not say; but it may well have been a reflection on his conduct towards his brother, who was suspected of having hastened Titus' death. Besides, he could not forgive Titus for having been brought up at court along with Britannicus, whose fate he narrowly escaped, whereas Domitian had been fostered in mean seclusion. He found consolation in infamy. It was said that Nerva (who was to succeed him) had enjoyed his youthful favours. He was idle and coarse. He was also pathologically bloodthirsty. A curious incident shows how in his day, lewdness could vindicate loyalty. A handsome and noble young officer called Julius Calvaster was reported to have had frequent meetings alone with Antonius, who, as governor of Germany, revolted against Domitian. Antonius was speedily destroyed. Julius had no other way of freeing himself from the charge of conspiracy than by asserting that his only dealings with Antonius had been erotic. The admission secured his acquittal.

Titus had wanted Domitian to marry his own daughter, Julia. Domitian turned her down. To such a warped and vengeful youth, the seduction of another man's wife for what he called 'bed-wrestling' was more attractive than honest matrimony. Thus it was that he acquired Domitia, the daughter of the brilliant and unhappy General Corbulo. Domitia was married to an illustrious senator called Lamia. In the prim words of the honourable Bysse Molesworth (1752): "This lady was too much of a coquette to confine her inclinations within the narrow limits of conjugal fidelity, for by the loss of her father whom Nero (that enemy of all virtue) sacrificed to his brutal fury she was deprived of all those good examples and lessons which he had been very assiduous in giving her, and her ambition, added to her natural inclination to amours, turned the daughter of the wisest and greatest of men into the most abandoned and debauched courtesan in Rome." Or as Molesworth's contemporary Samuel Johnson put it when Boswell was trying to excuse a well-born adulteress: "the woman's a whore, and there's an end on't". Domitia and Domitian were birds of a feather. As soon as he was emperor, Domitian forced Lamia to divorce his wife and married her himself.

The niece whom he had spurned, Julia, was later married to an eminent consular called Sabinus. Domitian at once fell violently in love with her, although Domitia had already borne him a daughter. Domitia, nothing daunted, gave herself up to lechery. In particular, she was enamoured of an actor called Paris. Domitian had him murdered in broad daylight, as well as those who honoured his memory at the place where he had been slain. Even a young and ailing pupil of the actor was killed because he looked like his master. Sabinus was soon got rid of, and Domitian could enjoy Julia unmolested. He thought of killing Domitia, but was dissuaded by a friend, and divorced her instead. Julia, finding herself pregnant, was compelled by Domitian to attempt abortion, which caused her death. She was duly deified.

Domitian, pretending that it was 'the people's wish', now took back his Domitia, probably in the year 84. She rewarded her husband by joining a conspiracy to murder him. He used to say that the lot of princes was unhappy indeed, because when they discovered a conspiracy no one believed them until they were dead. So it turned out in Domitian's case. He had a niece called Domitilla, whose steward Stephanus lay under a charge of embezzlement. Now that Domitian had become a compulsive killer, it was obvious that Stephanus would be doomed unless he and Domitia's friends struck first. And not only Stephanus. Domitilla was married to a cousin, a slack, easy-going man called Clemens. He had so far kept in favour to the extent that Domitian had proclaimed two of their children his successors, naming them Vespasian and Domitian and had appointed Quintillian their tutor. Scarcely has Clemens laid down his consulate in 95, than he and his wife were accused of 'atheism', probably because they favoured the Jewish or Christian way of life. Clemens was executed, Domitilla banished. If such eminent relations could be so treated, who was safe? No one, low or high. We learn from Epictetus that *agents provocateurs* were sent into the circus, to pose as critics of the régime. If their neighbours showed any signs of agreeing, they were at once arrested and put away. Domitia saw that she must act and act quickly. The little frightened cabal did what no previous plotters, from those who slew Julius Caesar up to their own day, had done: they looked ahead, they planned. Seneca had once said to Nero: "Remember that however many men you kill, you cannot kill your successor." Domitia and her friends had a successor ready, a respected old senator called Nerva. At first he thought they were setting a trap for him; but once they had convinced him, he agreed to occupy the perilous eminence they offered. For some time Stephanus wore his right arm in a bandage, in which he concealed a dagger. After a few days no-one noticed it any more. Then, on the 18th September 96, Stephanus after greeting Domitian, whipped out the dagger and stabbed his unsuspecting quarry. Others added lethal blows, and Stephanus himself was killed by those who came to Domitian's aid.

Dio tells us that he 'heard tell' the following account of how Domitian's end was precipitated. It was the custom, he says, for Roman nobles to keep in their households little boys, human *putti*, who ran about naked but for a few jewels, and whose office it was to amuse their masters by their prattle and pretty ways. Domitian had such a little fellow, who had the freedom of his bedchamber. On the fateful 18th September, he went in to it as his master was having his siesta, and saw at the bed's head, a tablet, with writing on it. Picking it up, he ran out into the corridor, where he met Domitia. Taking the tablet from his little hands, the empress started to read it. To her horror, she learned, by the means of this innocent messenger, the list of those who were marked for death, with her own name at the top. No time was to be lost. The cabal assembled, and Domitian was despatched as he lay on his bed.

The story is of special interest, because it is repeated almost word for word in the description of the death of Commodus, with Marcia playing the part of Domitia. Such an occurrence is hardly to be credited as having happened twice. It is anyone's guess as to when it actually did. Balsdon gives it to Commodus; and probability inclines to that context, if only because it is clear that in the case of Domitian, Stephanus had been preparing 'for some time' to strike the blow which in the event he did.

Domitia had won, and won far more than she expected to win. Not only did she live for another forty years, but she had unwittingly moulded a century of peace and glory for the Eternal City. Apart from her length of life we hear no more of her; but we have already heard enough to place her among the most successful women in history. She created an era.

CHAPTER VIII

The Spanish Emperors

THE APPOINTMENT OF Nerva as emperor was a stroke of unconscious genius. Nerva was a senator, and an old man too. His elevation was a positive denial of the divine right of the soldiers to rule Rome. The new emperor came of a family which had long been eminent and was remotely connected on both sides with the Julio-Claudians. Nerva was one of Vespasian's first candidates for the consulate. He had no sons to succeed him and had never apparently held any military or provincial command, and so was free from the jealous rancour of disappointed rivals. His nature was mild and benevolent, so much so that his first consul, Fronto, a distinguished jurist, was heard to say that it was bad enough to have had a ruler under whom no-one could do anything, but worse to have one under whom anybody could do everything. Taken all in all, the short reign—only sixteen months—of this elderly civilian did seem to fulfil the wish which Cicero had uttered in one of his own verses: 'Cedant arma togae', 'let arms give place to civilian array.' The coins tell us the official story. 'The Justice of Augustus', 'The slander of the Jewish tax removed', meaning that only self-confessed Jews need now pay the tax imposed after the capture of Jerusalem, 'Rome reborn', 'Public Liberty'. The food-supply was assured, the water-supply improved and regulated; financial aid was given to indigent minors.

The praetorians, despite their having received the usual bribe, were resentful; and their commander, who had held the post under Domitian, was still brutally determined to show Nerva that it was the army which ruled. He therefore demanded what

can justly be regarded as the 'extradition' from the charmed
circle of the court of two men whom he knew to be intimate
friends of the emperor, on the ground that they had conspired
against Domitian. He succeeded, too: the men were handed
over, despite all Nerva's entreaties, and were soon executed.
Nerva saw at once that he could not face the world of Roman
intrigue alone. He must have a 'Caesar'—the word having now
lost its genealogical connotation, and become a courtesy title for
the heir apparent. Nerva's choice was a magnificently bold one.
Did the soldiers insist that they ruled Rome? Well, he would
trump their ace, by appointing as his successor the most eminent
soldier of them all. He therefore ascended the Capitol, and
gathering all his strength, proclaimed in a loud voice: "May
good fortune attend the Roman Senate and myself. I hereby
adopt Marcus Ulpius Nerva Trajan," including his own name
in the title to seal the adoption. The choice was immediately
ratified by the Senate.

Nerva's declaration opened a completely new epoch in the
affairs of imperial Rome. Hitherto Rome itself had been the
centre of all policy and action. For more than eight hundred
years it was from Rome that life and light had radiated. Gradually
all Italy had become her domain, then Sicily, then Greece, Asia
Minor, the Levant, Gaul. Finally even Spain, which had first
known Roman arms in the age of the Scipios, at the end of the
third century BC, had become a Roman dominion, though it had
not been completely subdued until the days of Augustus himself.
Once conquered it became Rome's richest single province. It
produced gold, silver, lead, copper, and the only known vein of
mica which, until the improvement of glass, was the sole refined
glazing material. Its corn was abundant, its wines choice. Above
all, it was framed on a larger scale than any region of Italy. Not
even the grand expanse of the Po valley can equal the wide
undulating plains of Spain, especially in Andalusia, from which
both Trajan and Hadrian sprang. Even today the wayfarer is
deceived into believing that the cities are nearer to each other
than they really are. That feature of the country, and its division
by lofty mountain ranges into regions which hardly knew each
other, made as ever in Spanish history for a separatism, an intense
individuality, unknown in Italy. Moreover southern Spain is
nearer, more in contact with, Northern Africa than with the
rest of Europe. Throughout history this geographical setting has

had a profound influence on the inhabitants of Spain. Even in the second century, the Spanish Romans talked with a provincial accent, as Hadrian was to find to his cost when he first entered public life in Rome. The Romans laughed at him.

Nerva had passed over not only Romans, but Italians, and Italiots, inhabitants, that is, of the many Greek cities in southern Italy.

Spain had already given Rome men of talent, but chiefly in the realm of letters. The Senecas, father and son, Quintillian, Lucan, Martial, Pomponius Mela the geographer, Columella who wrote on agriculture, all hailed from Spain, as did more than one lawyer of repute. Above all, these Spanish-born or -descended Romans had, as we should expect, a wider outlook than those who knew only Rome. They were all loyal to 'Romanitas', but instead of looking in on it, they tended to look outwards, and to wish to implant that very concept abroad. It was against this background that arose Roman Spain's most famous sons, Trajan and his relative and successor Hadrian.

To our great loss, our written information about either of them is scrappy. We are almost wholly dependent on what Gibbon described as "the glimmerings of an abridgement and the doubtful light of a panegyric".

As soon as Nerva had made his pronouncement and had secured the Senate's ratification of it, he wrote to Trajan who was governor of Germany at the time in his own hand adding a quotation from Homer which he knew would please Trajan. The new Caesar had little formal education, but like many men of action fostered in others the graces he himself lacked. Within three months Nerva was dead. He had long been ailing. He suffered from chronic stomachic debility, which induced incessant vomiting, to such a degree that an astrologer had assured Domitian that although Nerva had been born with a royal horoscope, he was not worth murdering because he would soon be dead anyway.

Trajan was now emperor. He was at Cologne when the news came. His first recorded act as ruler was to send for the rebellious guardsmen and their commander, under the pretext of wishing to entrust them with a special commission. For one thing, he was bound to avenge his 'father', but the major consideration was that he make it plain at the very outset of his rule that the emperor commanded the Guard, and not they the emperor. They were duly executed. Trajan was now in the prime of life, forty-

Empress Sabina, the wife of Hadrian, a bust in the Vatican Museum

a) Sabina

b) Hadrian

c) Empress Crispina, wife of Commodus

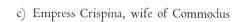

six, the same age as Wellington when he won the battle of Waterloo. He was no stranger to Rome, having been consul in 91; but his extended military service had kept him away from the capital long enough for him to have escaped the hot-house intrigues of Domitian's reign. When in 99 he entered Rome on foot, he was welcomed by the citizens with relief and rapture. With him was his wife Plotina. She had been born at Nîmes and belonged to a family of some local distinction. She was modest, morally without blemish, but, as her portraits suggest, a clever, far-sighted woman. She was interested in religion and in philosophy, favouring the Epicurean school. She was the ideal mate for Trajan.

A happy throng of citizens attended the imperial couple to the Palatine. When they reached the top of the stairway by which they had ascended from the Forum, Plotina turned round, and, greatly daring, addressed the populace. "I hope," she said, "that when the time comes for me to leave this building, I shall be the same woman as I am today." The Romans treasured this remark. It seems rather commonplace to us, but it meant a very great deal to the Romans for two reasons. The first is that it proclaimed a patently sincere intention to preserve or more correctly, to return to an era of decency such as Rome had not known since the days of Livia, who had died seventy years before. The second is that since the days of Augustus the palace had never been what a palace should be, the centre and summit of social life. Trajan made it as clear as Plotina had done that he regarded the palace as the property of the Roman people. So few citizens had ever been inside it. Even the good Vespasian spent most of his time in the Gardens of Sallust, upon the Quirinal, as another 'good' emperor, Aurelian was to do in the next century. Now it would once again be used and lived in. Or rather the new palace would be. The original *palatium* was small and pokey. It was also both noisy and smelly. It stood directly above the Forum, which besides housing the Vestal Virgins and the Senate, was a teeming commercial centre. Shops, booths and taverns stood there, alongside the temples and shrines, citizens chattered and chaffered, flies were everywhere. Tiberius' additions, handsome as they were, only brought the palace nearer to the Forum; and those underground passages, such as Nero constructed, must have been as dank and eerie as they are today. It was Domitian who, with all his faults, set about the construction of an entirely new

H

palace at the southern end of the hill, that is as far away from the
din as possible. Fortunately an original and very capable architect
was at hand, Rabirius, a friend of the poet Martial. The setting
is spacious, the main buildings facing south across a delightful
piazza to the Alban Hills, at the foot of which Domitian had
his favourite country-house. The general lay-out suggests Eastern
influences. The throne-room opens directly onto the square, just
like a Persian *liwan*. The vault has a span of over one hundred
feet. (We are apt to think of vaults as peculiarly Gothic; but
the widest Gothic vault, that of the cathedral of Gerona in
Spain, is seventy-three feet: the widest in England, that of the
former Lady Chapel at Ely, is only forty-six.) Oriental-style
fountains flank the piazza, to soothe the ears no less than the
eyes, the water being conveyed from the Caelian hill by a branch
of the Aqua Claudia. There is a sunk garden, too, in the shape
of a miniature hippodrome, with colonnades. This charming
creation became known as the *Domus Augustana*, the home of the
emperors. While Plotina presided in it, how eager would the
Romans be to visit her.

With the Spanish emperor and his model wife we enter an
entirely fresh stratum of history, for two reasons. The first is that
they and their relations seem so 'modern', so post-Proustian. It
would be hard to imagine, say Mauriac or Galsworthy, assembling
a masterly little world, such as they display for us in their 'family'
novels, with Caligula or Agrippina or Domitian as living beings,
motivated by psychological concepts. Whereas when we come to
the Spaniards, we certainly can. Secondly, as in the modern
'psychological' novel, no single character can be comprehended
without intimate connexion with others, just as life is, in fact,
lived. Thus it is impossible to write of Plotina without taking
in the lives of her relations, and in a special degree those of
Trajan's successor Hadrian and his wife Sabina.

Hadrian's father was a compatriot and first cousin of Trajan.
All we know of Hadrian's mother is that she was Domitia Paulina,
good Roman names both, and that she came from Gades, later
Cadiz. She may have had Iberian blood in her veins, or even
Irish; because the links between southern Spain and Hibernia
were strong. (They still are: during the summer fishing season,
the Spanish flag is prominent in Bantry Bay.) Trajan and Hadrian
both sprang from the town of Italica, now Santeponce, five miles
to the west of Seville. The original settlers were a community of

veteran Roman soldiers, planted there by Scipio Africanus after
he had driven the Carthaginians from Spain, in 205 BC. The
Hadrians had come from the city of Hadria, in Picenum, the
district on the north-east of Italy which fronts the Adriatic or
Hadriatic sea. The name chosen for the new town, Italica, under-
lines the attachment of the newcomers to their native land. The
visible remains of Italica show that it was a fine city, covering
130 acres, the equivalent of Mayfair and St James's put together.
The streets are wide, the amphitheatre the fourth largest in the
whole empire.

When Hadrian was ten, his father died. Even if his mother
were still alive, he would need guardians. Young Hadrian was
naturally committed to the charge of the most influential available,
which meant his cousin Trajan, and a knight called Attianus.
Hadrian's brother-in-law, Servianus, who was thirty-four years
older than Hadrian, wrote to Trajan about him, saying that he did
nothing but go hunting, and that he had run into debt. Trajan's
reaction was the very opposite of that which Servianus had desired:
he summoned his ward to Rome, and was at once captivated by
his handsome young cousin, who was soon launched on a military
career.

The relationship between Trajan and Hadrian is enigmatic.
We are told that "Trajan treated him like a son". Then why,
when the time came, and Hadrian was twenty-four, did he
oppose the marriage which Plotina arranged for him with Sabina,
Trajan's great-niece? The answer may be found in a sentence of
the *Augustan History*. "He was in the love of Trajan, and yet
owing to the activity of the guardians of certain boys whom
Trajan loved ardently, he was not free from . . . which Gallus
fostered." A word is missing from this tantalising sentence: it
may have been 'jealousy' or 'resentment'. What is clear is that
Trajan who was well known to prefer the intimacy of his own
sex, saw in Hadrian a handsome charmer who outshone all the
others. Plotina saw that too. Being more acute in affairs of the
heart than her husband, she determined to bring Hadrian into
the inner circle of power. She was, besides, very much attracted
to him. Hadrian was a prismatic character. He loved the pleasures
and perils of the chase, he painted, he sang, he was a sculptor
and a poet. He was so fond of the classics that he was nicknamed
Greekling. As an architect he was to win abiding renown. Roman
by birth and breeding, Greek by inclination he was not seldom

torn between the two strains, in an almost schizophrenic imbalance. He could be calm, just and indefatigably industrious, the 'universal genius' as the historian H. A. L. Fisher was to call him; but when he was opposed, or captivated, he could be callous, even cruel, or lascivious and vain. And, like most Romans, he was pathologically superstitious.

Plotina was not alone in her perception: others saw equally clearly that Hadrian stood so well with Trajan, that it would be prudent to stand well with Hadrian. When after Domitian's assassination, Trajan was chosen as Nerva's Caesar, his brother officers realised this as well as anyone: and so it was Hadrian whom they sent to bear their congratulations to the heir apparent. When Trajan became emperor in three months, Hadrian once again hastened to congratulate his cousin, now sovereign of the Roman world. His brother-in-law once again showed his jealousy. He tried to detain Hadrian, and when the young man insisted in going on, arranged that his travelling-carriage should break down. Hadrian finished the journey on foot. Trajan was pleased. Hadrian never forgot Servianus' malignity.

When Trajan arrived in Rome in 99, Hadrian was at his side. He was twenty-four. Plotina was fonder of Hadrian even than Trajan was. She perfectly understood that Trajan would oppose any marriage for Hadrian. He wanted Hadrian for himself, and did not relish the idea of sharing him with anyone, especially a wife. But Plotina realised that to fortify Hadrian's position as prospective heir, it was essential that he marry into the family. Plotina was not only a modest woman, but a very clever one as well. Her portraits show a pensive face, with a determined mouth, and an air of introspection, of melancholy almost. (They also show the extravagant coiffure which had become the fashion; though compared with some of her contemporaries, Plotina's was almost dowdy.)

In the year 100 Pliny the younger, Trajan's friend, delivered in the Senate in gratitude for his election as consul a panegyric of which the text has been preserved to us. This is what he says of Plotina (Balsdon's translation):

Many men of importance have incurred discredit because they rushed into marriage with too little thought, or because they were too complaisant in tolerating a wife whom they would have done well to divorce; the discredit they incurred in their private lives effaced the distinction of their public careers, and because they were unable to control their wives at home, they were thought to fall below the standard of the perfect Roman.

Your wife on the other hand has brought you nothing but renown and distinction. No woman alive has greater integrity or represents more perfectly the best tradition of Roman womanhood. If the High Priest had to choose a wife, she—or some woman like her—would be his certain choice.

Some woman like her, do I say? But where is there such another woman?

Here, at least, there is no exaggeration. A further tribute is paid to Plotina—in that she and her sister-in-law lived under the same roof in perfect harmony. Indeed, not only Marciana but Plotina too deserves this praise. By the year 105, both Plotina and Marciana, who had at first declined the honorific of Augusta, accepted it. In 112 they were both given the right to issue coins. In his peroration, Pliny utters the following striking prayer:

First I beseech thee [Jupiter] that if he govern the republic well, and for the common good, thou mayest be pleased to preserve him unto our nephews and great-nephews; and that finally thou wilt grant unto him a successor born of his seed, formed by him and made like unto his adopted son, or if this be forbidden by fate, that thou mayest direct his choice, and mayest shew unto him one worthy to be adopted in the Capitol.

These words, uttered on the morrow of Hadrian's marriage to Trajan's great-niece, are a pretty clear indication that one of Trajan's friends at least hoped that Hadrian would succeed his great-uncle as emperor.

Plotina from her long association with Trajan, and her affection for Hadrian, quite well understood that they both had the same sexual inclinations. Being a sensible woman, she had taken two from four, and had found that two still remained; in other words that a shared throne was worth an unshared bed. Why should not Hadrian's wife do the same? Unfortunately, Sabina did not see it that way at all. The marriage was disastrous. Hadrian never cared for her. As her portraits show, she was a feckless, listless woman. The tight little mouth betokens a weakness that would

always prefer private hostility to open opposition. She is reported
to have said that she would never bear a child to perpetuate so
inhuman a character. Their antipathy was mutual. Hadrian
found her a sulky shrew. Were he an ordinary citizen he would
have divorced her, he said. Nevertheless he insisted that as his
consort she must be treated as such. While he was in Britain, he
heard that Suetonius the biographer, who was at the time his
private secretary, and a prefect of the Guard had treated Sabina
with undue familiarity. They were both dismissed. Hadrian
tolerated Sabina, and she held to him. But we cannot tell how
often she accompanied him on his endless journeys.

Plotina's greatest achievement came in the year 117. Trajan
at the age of sixty, after an interval of seven peaceful years,
during which, in conjunction with Plotina we may be sure, he
had constructed the great complex of his forum, his column,
and the libraries and markets to set it off, to be renowned as a
world's wonder till the end of time, had set out for the east, in
Balsdon's words, "to command the most ambitious enterprise of
unprovoked aggression since the disaster of Crassus in 53 BC".
Plotina and Matidia, Sabina's mother, and Hadrian went with
him; but not Sabina. All along the route arches and statues
sprang up like mushrooms, even in islands as remote as Rhodes
and Crete. Some honoured Trajan, others Plotina.

Trajan left the ladies at Antioch, and went to the front. At
first he was successful, he captured Ctesiphon, and made his
way right down to the Persian Gulf. Then he heard that in his
wake many of those whom he thought he had subdued had
rebelled. Back he must go. Then in the winter of 116/117 he
had a stroke. He must now go home, to Rome. During the
ensuing months his health grew rapidly worse. Plotina was deeply
distressed at the awful prospect of losing Trajan; but she realised
too what a grave responsibility now rested on her shoulders,
nothing less than Rome's future. Hadrian was left behind to
govern Syria. Only Matidia and Attianus were with her. The
end came at a little town in Cilicia, the port of Selinous, now
Selente, opposite Cyprus.

As usual, Plotina knew what to do. It had been obvious for
some time that Hadrian was the most likely heir and successor.
Many had been the auguries in his favour. During the second
Dacian war, in 105, Hadrian had greatly distinguished himself.
Trajan not only paid for the 'games' which Hadrian gave on his

return, but presented him with a diamond ring, which he, Trajan, had received from Nerva. Such a gift recalled that when the great Augustus was apparently at death's door, he had sent for his minister Agrippa and had formally bestowed upon him his signet-ring. That Hadrian now possessed a ring which had belonged to two successive emperors could mean only one thing. Hadrian was promoted praetor, and then at the age of thirty-three, after governing what is now eastern Hungary, he was nominated consul. While he held that office one of Trajan's most trusted generals, a Spaniard called Sura, had told Hadrian that he was to be adopted. There he was, the ward, the favourite, the nephew by marriage of the emperor who had given him the symbolic ring—it was clearly his destiny to succeed to the purple. How clever Plotina had been. She knew that Hadrian had many enemies in Rome. To proclaim adoption prematurely might wreck the whole design. Then in the year 112 came a highly-charged compliment from Athens itself. Its citizens elected Hadrian as their 'archon' or ruler. They had, it is true, elected Domitian, but he was a reigning emperor; never before had they elected a foreign commoner. This election is the clearest sign we have that not only in the Court, but in the wider world, Hadrian was regarded as the heir.

Now came the crisis. Sura who might have arranged these things, was now dead. Plotina coped with it as though she had long foreseen it, as indeed she must have done.

On 9th August news reached Hadrian in Syria that he had been adopted, and a declaration to that effect, witnessed by Plotina, had been sent to the Senate at Rome. Two days later, on the 11th, Hadrian received a second despatch, informing him that Trajan was dead.

What had happened? How was it done? Had Trajan really adopted Hadrian? Or had Plotina contrived the whole thing? The only competent witness, Trajan's valet, died the next day. From natural causes or because he knew too much? No one has ever known the truth. All sorts of stories went about. The silliest was that Plotina, having hidden Trajan's corpse, smuggled someone into the darkened bedchamber, who, with his head all muffled up, had imitated Trajan's feeble voice, and declared that Hadrian was his 'son'. Of this laughable device Puccini might make an operatic farce, but it does not fit real life. Plotina would know better. This long-sighted woman must have made her plans in good time; she would not be the last woman to influence political affairs for a husband no longer capable of doing so. Dio, who is in general hostile to Hadrian, says that his father, who was governor of Cilicia sixty years later, used to say that Trajan's death was concealed for several days, and that Plotina forged the warrant of adoption and signed it herself. Trajan being paralysed, who else could sign it? As the principate of Hadrian, and of the two successors he himself chose, provided the last Golden Age imperial Rome was to know, Plotina's ruse, if ruse it was, was one which only malevolence could impugn. Gratitude would be a more becoming emotion.

Plotina and Matidia, with Attianus as escort, carried the ashes back to Rome. Hadrian himself had accompanied them on board.

Matidia died within two years of Hadrian's accession. Plotina lived only two or three years longer. Marciana, who had died in 112, was like the two others, duly deified.

When Plotina died Hadrian appeared in deep mourning for nine days. She was honoured by a temple at Nîmes her birthplace. In pronouncing her funeral oration Hadrian said, "She often made requests of me, and I never refused her anything." Such was the lifelong moderation of this 'most irreproachable of women' as Pliny once described her, and such the mutual love which united one of Rome's finest daughters to one of Rome's ablest sons.

It is with a feeling akin to aversion that we must inspect, however briefly, the marital bondage of Hadrian. Plotina had acted in what she considered to be Hadrian's and Rome's interest; but not even Plotina could chasten the temper of Sabina. Perhaps she never intended to? Perhaps that was why Marciana and Matidia had sided with her, so that Plotina should have no rival for Hadrian's love, nor Trajan either? She was granted the title Augusta in 128, when Hadrian accepted that of Father of the Fatherland. Two years later Sabina was certainly with him when he visited Egypt. The party which went up the Nile on that occasion was a curious one. There was Hadrian, with Sabina, Antinoüs and Balbilla. Antinoüs was Hadrian's famous Bithynian favourite, who lost his life by drowning in the river. That the relations between Hadrian and Antinoüs were carnal was commonly believed—even Julian repeats the slur in his satire on the Caesars. The evidence does not support that view. Hadrian would be the last man to flaunt so disreputable a liaison. Antinoüs most probably drowned himself, hoping thereby not only to achieve godhead—for, in ancient Egypt, persons drowned in the Nile were believed to secure it—but to help his beloved master, who was already showing signs of physical decline. All over the empire the dead boy was venerated, often assimilated to Hermes, Apollo or some Egyptian deity. A whole new city, Antinoöpolis arose near the spot where he had been drowned. Most notable of all is the fact that Sabina is never known to have objected to Antinoüs. On the contrary, the granite obelisk which now stands on the Pincio in Rome is a family memorial. It bears the names of Hadrian, Sabina and Antinoüs. He is depicted in a relief at the base as receiving the 'ankh', symbol of life, at the hands of the god Tot.

Sabina's companion on this fatal tour was a woman called Balbilla. She regarded herself as a poetess. The party went to hear the famous 'singing' statue of Memnon (really of Amenophis II, 1442–1416 BC.) It was one of a pair, and in Hadrian's day was still entire. The statues face the dawn. As the rising sun warmed the more northerly effigy, the expanding stone gave forth a griding noise 'like the snapping of a taut harpstring'. Twice the imperial party visited the statue and heard it 'sing'. Balbilla recorded the event in five dreadful little poems in Aeolic Greek, of all ridiculous dialects, which she had engraved on Memnon's left foot. The god, says Balbilla, greeted Hadrian before sunrise (which was impossible) and twice again later. Hadrian returned the greeting, and everyone could see how dear he was to the gods. One doubts though whether Balbilla was very dear to Hadrian. Was that why Sabina had invited her?

Poor Sabina! She may have been all that Hadrian said of her; he may have deserved all the reproaches she spread abroad about him. They never loved each other, but she stuck to him. She was deified. A touching monument now in the Museo dei Conservatori on the Capitol depicts her deification. Every metre that carries her farther away from Hadrian, who is watching with extreme unconcern, brings her nearer heaven. Let us hope she saw it like that.

CHAPTER IX

'Equanimity' and Chaos

WHEN TRAJAN WARNED his friend the younger Pliny who, as governor of Bithynia had come into conflict with the Christians, that he was not to countenance informers or anonymous dela- tions, he added that any wanton persecution was a 'very bad example and unworthy of our time'.

He meant it, and was justified in meaning it. Trajan was conscious that he really had been the pioneer of a new age. Plotina had influenced him in his policy. It was Plotina who had urged him to be stricter in his punishment of corruption; Plotina who had persuaded him to befriend the Jews of Alexandria against their pagan accusers. Hadrian, as emperor, carried on this mild and decent attitude, again, beyond doubt modelling his conduct on the exhortations of his revered Plotina. He was even persuaded to relax the rule which required that the head of the Epicurean school at Athens must be a Roman citizen.

It is given to few men to rule from the grave, yet it might almost be said of Hadrian that he succeeded in doing it. Plotina must be awarded her fair share in that posthumous invigilation. To what extent she really did influence policy, what the main- springs of men's actions were, we can only guess. Charles Tennyson in his life of his grandfather records that Edmund Gosse saw Lord Tennyson stop in front of a bust of Antinoüs in the British Museum and say in his deep slow voice: "Ah, this is the in- scrutable Bithynian. If we knew what he knew, we should understand the ancient world."

Our knowledge of the ancient world in the age of Antinoüs and after is still almost as bounded as it was in Tennyson's day. As we approach the fascinating and formative age of the Antonines, the age of gold as those who knew it and its succeeding era were to remember it, more and more we feel the utter frustration of the lack of any reliable literary sources. The epitome of Dio, the mysterious and all too often misleading gallimaufry of the Augustan lives—we have almost nothing beside these two frail props to sustain the burden of history. This is all the more tantalising when we recall that for a single day in the year 69, 15th January, we have no less than four accounts of the death of Galba, those of Tacitus, Suetonius, Plutarch and Dio, and that each is in harmony with the others.

Hadrian had decided that in one particular he would deviate from Plotina's régime. Sabina was not to be trusted, even if she had the wit for an emergency. Besides she might—and in the event did—die before him. Hadrian was determined that the succession should be absolutely assured, cast iron, fool-proof. The method by which he achieved it was extremely complex. His first choice of Lucius Ceionius is inexplicable except on the assumption that he was a natural son of Hadrian, or that Hadrian was his lover. Fortunately this singularly unqualified candidate died before Hadrian. The second choice was excellent: the emperor we know as Antoninus Pius, the ruler who gave his name to an age, a name which would be assumed without any just title even by rulers who succeeded that age. Hadrian peered ahead into the mists of yet a second generation. To be the joint successors of Antoninus, Hadrian chose the man who is famous as Marcus Aurelius (who was first nephew, then adopted son, then son-in-law of Antoninus) and Lucius Verus (who was first adoptive brother and then son-in-law of Marcus Aurelius.) A dynastic bond was thus preserved in the Antonine fabric.

We must ever be on our guard against slicing up history into 'reigns' as was for so long done in English history-books. True, a new reign does sometimes inaugurate a new age. Trajan is a case in point, and so is our own King Charles II. But in general, history is not a succession of lantern-slides, each projected separately; it is a kaleidoscope. It is for ever turning; it is only when we hear the click of its components and behold a new pattern that we realise that we are looking at the same elements in a new formation. This is particularly true of the Antonine age, which is in so many respects a continuation of the age of Trajan, Plotina and Hadrian, especially of the last who had taken such

meticulous precautions to ensure that his own views of government should be perpetuated. They were too. In the *Augustan
History* there are more than thirty references to Hadrian in the
narratives of later emperors, right through a century after his
death. It was Dio, who had no love for Hadrian, who contrasted
the age of gold with the succeeding age of iron and rust which he
had lived to endure.

The Antonine age was in reality the prolongation of the
Trajan-Hadrian creation, when, in the words of the elder Pliny,
the world was lapped in 'the infinite majesty of the Roman
peace'.

Even the ethnic strains of Gaul and Spain had endured.
Antoninus' ancestors had come, like Plotina, from Nîmes. His
wife, ten or twelve years younger than himself, was Annia Galeria
Faustina, known as the elder Faustina. Her family came from
southern Spain. Thus the Ibero-Gallic *côterie* was to rule Rome
after Hadrian's death.

We have some details, despite meagre sources, about the
emperors Antoninus and Marcus: we know, *grosso modo*, what
they were like and what they did. Their wives on the other hand,
provide, as wives so often do, an insoluble enigma.

The elder Faustina, it is true, shared the throne with Antoninus
for only three years. Their daughter, the younger Faustina was
already betrothed to Marcus Aurelius. She had first been destined
for Lucius Verus, who was only eight at the time; so Antoninus,
possibly with Hadrian's consent, switched her to Marcus
Aurelius who was seventeen. Hadrian was devoted to the
studious boy—he enlarged his patronymic Verus to 'Verissimus',
the truest. In the end Lucius Verus married one of their
daughters.

The reason for the mystery that cloaks the Faustinae is this:
posterity daubed them both with pitch; and yet few women have
stood higher in the estimation of their contemporaries, including
both blameless husbands. Emperors, Senate, inscriptions and
coins all treat them as women of integrity. Honour upon honour
was poured out upon them. For instance, whereas Sabina had
had to wait ten years before being named Augusta, the elder
Faustina by a vote of the Senate which her husband approved,
was given that honourable augmentation on her husband's
succession. When she died after only three years as empress she
was buried in Hadrian's mausoleum (now Castel Sant' Angelo,

and the setting of the last act of Puccini's *Tosca*). She was consecrated, to become *diva Faustina Augusta*. A temple was built and dedicated to her—originally to her alone; but when her consort died the practical Romans simply added his name to hers in the inscription. We can still read it. The temple is still there, on the Via Sacra, to the right as you go down to the senate-house, having had the good fortune to be reconsecrated as the Christian church of S. Lorenzo in Miranda. Its frieze houses some of the finest bas-reliefs in all Roman sculpture. It strongly influenced Renaissance and later neo-classical artists, so that Faustina has achieved a more abiding memorial than any other empress. A handsome reward for three years' work. But the temple, fine as it is, was not to be Faustina's only guerdon. An extensive coinage, bearing the legend 'Aeternitas'—eternity—was issued, thus making her part of the 'Eternal City' whose nine hundredth anniversary was soon to be celebrated.

Thirdly, and most humanly, to revivify one of Trajan's best institutions, an endowment was established to assist impoverished young girls—*puellae Faustinianae*, they were called.

It is hard to believe that such a woman, beloved by such a man, was a wanton. Dio does not mention her, or to be more accurate his epitome which is all we possess of him at this juncture is silent regarding her.

The Augustan history which duly records her honours and benefactions alone denigrates her, and that in a single sentence, which cites no factual evidence and is besides a patent interpolation. The context is as follows (III, 6):

While setting out to assume his proconsular office he lost his elder daughter [Aurelia Fadilla: her sepulchral inscription is preserved]. About the licence and loose living of his wife a number of things were said, which he heard with great sorrow and suppressed. On returning from his proconsulship he lived for the most part in Rome, being a member of Hadrian's privy council, and in all matters concerning which Hadrian sought his advice, ever urging the more merciful course.

This paragraph (like those which precede and follow it) is obviously part of a record of Antoninus' *curriculum vitae*. What writer in his senses would slip in an irrelevant aside about the empress's morals between his setting out for his province (Asia) and his return from it? None. Whoever wrote that piece of spiteful falsehood condemns himself (or herself?), not Faustina. It is simply a clumsy essay in chiaroscuro, the shadow being blackened to enhance the purity of the subject's high-lights.

When we come to the younger Faustina the analysis is by no means so easy. In 161 Antoninus died. He was universally regretted, not only by Marcus, who twice pays tribute to him in his *Meditations*—disinterested praise, worth having from such a man—but by the larger world. Sixteen years earlier, a polished Greek orator called Aristides was in Rome, having come by land from Smyrna along the great Via Egnatia in just under three weeks, a remarkably rapid transit. He reached the capital in time to celebrate the birthday of the city, which was, and still is, kept on 21st April. For 898 years the city had stood. In his oration there is naturally enough a good measure of flattery. But its whole tenor does leave upon the reader an impression of stability, continuity and liberalism. Rome, he says, is a partnership, not a despotism. "Neither sea nor intervening continent are bars to citizenship, nor are Asia and Europe treated differently in regard to it. In your empire all paths are open to all. No one worthy of rule or responsibility remains an alien, but a civil community of the world has been established as a free republic under one man, the best, the ruler and teacher of order." Antoninus died as he had lived, in tranquillity and dignity. He was seventy-four. Realising that his end had come, he gave orders that the golden statue of Fortune which the emperors always kept in their bedchambers as a sort of talisman should be committed to his adopted son and son-in-law Marcus Aurelius, as a symbol of his succession. When the officer of the day asked him for the watchword, "Equanimity," said Antoninus, "and so turning as if he would sleep, he ceased to breathe."

Marcus Aurelius was now emperor at the age of forty. He had long been trained for the supreme office. In 145 his marriage to the daughter of Antoninus and Faustina, his first cousin, was celebrated with glistening splendour, including a handsome bribe to the soldiers. Their first child was born a year later, whereupon both parents received outstanding public honours. Marcus was associated in the rule of Antoninus, and Faustina was granted the title of Augusta with the right to coin. That was after the birth of their first child, a daughter, 'Faustina the younger'. The marriage was to prove the most fruitful that any imperial family had ever known. Twelve or perhaps even more children did Faustina bear. This productivity was celebrated in the coinage: *Fecunditas Augustae* was the superscription. Many of the brood naturally died infants; but some survived, including two whom Rome would have been happier without, the future emperor Commodus and his older sister Lucilla, who was to marry Lucius Verus. Lucius was Marcus' adoptive brother, whom the emperor made his full partner, so that for the first time Rome had two Augusti at the helm. Lucius was lewd and *fainéant*. He was sent east to handle a Parthian invasion: it was exactly two hundred years since any Parthian had been seen west of the Euphrates except as a suppliant, a prisoner or a hostage. Lucius, in the face of this threat, which coincided with an equally serious one in the north, dallied and dawdled his way through Greece and Asia, sampling all the most agreeable spas and casinos. He reached Antioch in 163. There he found that the army had been re-organised by a capable martinet of Syrian origin, Avidius Cassius. This gifted schemer brought the campaign to a victorious conclusion. Verus then started for home again. By this time he was married to Lucilla, the third child of Marcus and Faustina, the wedding having been solemnised at Ephesus in 164. Lucius was thirty-four, his bride about sixteen. She was to lead one of the most unhappy lives of all the family. Verus behaved outrageously. His army had become infected with the plague which had caused the usual disastrous consequences, including acute financial stringency—Rome's imperial finances were always conducted on what a modern scholar has happily dubbed 'the Micawber principle' and he paid no heed to the comfort or reputation of his young wife, nor to the sagging economy. He gave extravagant and lascivious banquets. His favourite obsession was a Syrian actor called Memphius, whom he nicknamed 'Joy-Boy'. The troupe of actors and jugglers he brought back with him led the wits of Rome to say that in the east it had been pantomimes not Parthians who had been his quarry.

Meanwhile Marcus anxiously awaited his return, because the northern front demanded the immediate presence of both emperors. Avidius Cassius was left in charge of the east, as Hadrian had once been. It was to prove an ominous precedent. When they arrived at the scene of war, Verus wanted to break off the campaign, seduced by what the seventeenth-century translator of Herodian calls 'the sugred allectives' of Rome. Marcus yielded to him, and headed south. Fortunately for him and Rome, Verus was seized with apoplexy and died the next year at Altinum in the Veneto (now Altino, at the mouth of the Piave.) This meant that Lucilla was no longer empress, but a dowager who must yield precedence to her brother Commodus' wife, Crispina. This was unbearably galling to Lucilla. After all, she was Commodus' sister, and Commodus was now associated with Marcus in the direction of affairs, and was in effect crown prince. And Crispina was crown princess, while Lucilla was just a poor relation. She was hastily married off to an ageing nobleman called Pompeianus, by whom she had a son. Commodus in fact treated her with the greatest courtesy; but she could not forget her royal past, from which country life with Pompeianus was a rankling come-down. She allowed her jealousy and resentment to get the better of her wits. Commodus, as we learn from Herodian in his seventeenth-century guise, had 'bespurtled himself' beyond endurance, and lived chiefly for 'belly-cheere'. Poor Lucilla formed a plot together with a courtier called Ummidius Quadratus (and perhaps Paternus, the Guard commander) to kill Commodus. The plan was a good one, that Commodus be killed as he was entering the 'hunting-theatre', that is the Colosseum, where amid the surging throng, a relation of her second husband, who had been betrothed to Lucilla's daughter, and was alleged to have seduced not only the girl but Lucilla as well, was to step out from the shadows of the narrow vestibule and stab the emperor. When it came to the time for action, the youth lost his head and pointing a dagger at Commodus blurted out: "The Senate sends you this." The assassin *manqué*, together with the other plotters, and many others beside, were speedily despatched. Lucilla was first banished to Capri. So was Crispina, having, as Dio airly puts it, angered Commodus 'by some act of adultery'. She, too, was soon dead.

To return to Faustina, mother of Lucilla and of Commodus. Dio, when he reaches this period, specifically tells us: " I state these and subsequent facts, not, as hitherto, on the authority of others' reports, but from my own observation."

When it comes to Faustina's moral character, Dio has but a passing reference to her in his eulogy of Marcus, which could hardly be milder: "He refrained from all offences and did nothing amiss whether voluntarily or involuntarily; but the

a) Empress Faustina I, the deified wife of Antoninus Pius

b) Empress Faustina II, the wife of Marcus Aurelius

c) Crispina

a) Empress Julia Domna. The coin was struck in Rome by her husband, Septimius Severus. b) The reverse of the coin, showing her sons Caracalla and Geta, both of whom later became emperors

offences of others, particularly those of his wife, he tolerated, and neither enquired into them nor punished them."

Faustina's chief recorded error was political, and even then it was not really her fault. Realising that Marcus was becoming very frail, she decided to carry out a little 'insurance' with Avidius Cassius, and proposed that on Marcus' death she should become his wife and so keep the throne in the family, her excuse being that Commodus was too young—he was only fourteen—and somewhat simple-minded. Herodian adds the relevant argument that the succession of a minor might well incite the Germans to make more trouble. This, in itself, was not a bad idea. Commodus would naturally become Caesar, and in due course Augustus. Unfortunately the whole plan went awry owing to Avidius' believing a premature report of Marcus' death, upon which he declared himself emperor. Dio has Marcus make a long and altruistic speech, "never abusing Cassius in any way save that he constantly termed him ungrateful". He begged that none of his accomplices should be harmed. His only reaction to Cassius' attempt was to make the salutary rule that in future no one should serve as governor in his native province. Cassius was killed by the troops "after a dream of empire lasting three months and six days". Then Faustina died "either of the gout from which she suffered, or in some other manner, in order to avoid being convicted of her compact with Cassius". She died at Halala, at the foot of the Taurus mountains. The village was erected into a colony in her honour. Marcus was heart-broken at her death.

He had always loved her. He had lauded her in his *Meditations* as obedient, affectionate and devoid of affectation. Their friend Fronto (albeit he was an obsequious fraud) in writing to his former pupil Marcus refers to Faustina and the children as would be expected of a man writing to a happily married father of a family. Every possible honour was accorded Faustina after her death; she was called Mother of the Army and a golden statue was to take her accustomed place at public ceremonies in the theatre whenever the emperor himself was present. Silver images of Marcus and Faustina were set up in Hadrian's great temple of Venus and Rome at which engaged couples were to offer sacrifice.

How then can we account for the following interpolated paragraph (XXIX) in the *Augustan History*'s life of Marcus?

I

Some say, and it seems plausible, that Commodus Antoninus, his son and successor, was not begotten by him but in adultery; they embroider this assertion moreover with a story current among the people. On a certain occasion, it was said, Faustina the daughter of Pius and wife of Marcus saw some gladiators pass by, and was inflamed with love for one of them; and afterwards, when suffering from a long illness, she confessed the passion to her husband. And when Marcus reported this to the Chaldeans, it was their advice that the gladiator should be killed and that Faustina should bathe in his blood and thus couch with her husband. When this was done the passion was indeed allayed, but their son Commodus was born a gladiator, not really a prince; for afterwards as emperor he fought almost a thousand gladiatorian bouts before the eyes of the people, as shall be related in his life. The story is considered plausible, as a matter of fact, for the reason that the son of so virtuous a prince had habits worse than any play-actors, any fighter in the arena, or in fine, anything brought into existence from the offscourings of all dishonour and crime. Many writers, however, state that Commodus was really begotten in adultery, since it is generally known that Faustina, while at Caieta used to choose out lovers from among the sailors and gladiators. When Marcus was told this, that he might divorce, if not kill her, he is reported to have said, "If we send our wife away, we must also return her dowry"—meaning the empire.

The quip about the dowry is familiar—other emperors had used it before Marcus. This is only one of a ridiculous series of aspersions on Faustina's character. She is alleged to have had a string of lovers, from senators to actors, and to have been the subject of stage jokes. She is even credited with the murder of her son-in-law Verus by means of a dish of poisoned oysters, because the wretched dupe had confessed his guilty commerce with Faustina to her own daughter his wife!

The whole dirty catalogue is a pastiche of malice. But what was its intention? As Balsdon well puts it: "It was a story told with a purpose—to ensure that the reputation of Marcus Aurelius, who for the author of the *Lives* of the emperors was the hero of the whole series, should not be damaged by the fact of his having had such a man as Commodus for his son." There may well be a second reason. We do not know when, or in what circumstances,

the *Lives* were composed. It is generally believed that they are a
product of the late fourth or early fifth century. At the court of
Byzantium, (for some of the *Lives* pretend to be dedicated to
Constantine) or even of Diocletian, who had preceded Constantine's father in the west, and is also a dedicatee, it might well
have been imprudent to suggest that the court of the Antonines
had really been the purest and most golden on record, lest it
imply a cricitism of contemporary rulers. In days gone by (men
would recall) it had been a capital offence to be known as an
admirer of republican heroes, to make excerpts from Livy, for
instance, or keep a bust of Brutus in the hall. Be that as it may, to
Faustina we may justly apply Pope's lines:

> If to her share some female errors fall,
> Look on her face and you'll forget 'em all.

Like Antoninus, Marcus never remarried. Fabia to whom he had
been briefly betrothed as a youth, tried to capture him again.
But Marcus, very sensibly, took as his concubine an old family
friend, the daughter of one of Faustina's stewards 'so as not to
put a stepmother over his children.' He survived his wife by only
four years, and died, apparently of the plague, on March 17th,
in the year 180. He was one of Rome's most humane rulers. Any
form of bloodshed was abhorrent to him, even when it might be
legally justified. In the arena, he preferred to study state papers,
instead of watching the brutal performance: indeed, he would
permit only button-tipped foils to be used by the combatants;
and once when a tight-rope walker fell to his death, the emperor
commanded that in future—and his mandate has lasted to our
own time—all such acts should take place above a net. And it
was of this man that the silly tale related above was fabricated.

Commodus his son and successor reigned from 180, when he
was nineteen, until 192, when he was murdered, at the age of
thirty-one. That he was dissolute and despicable is not to be
denied, or rather that he became so. Once again, we must be
careful not to credit all that is said of him in the *Augustan History*.
Dio (if the epitome of Xiphilinus is to be trusted) starts his 72nd
Book as follows:

> This man [Commodus] was not naturally wicked, but on the
> contrary as guileless a man as ever lived. His great simplicity,
> however, together with his cowardice, made him the slave of

his companions, and it was through them that he at first, out
of ignorance, missed the better life and then was led on into
lustful and cruel habits, which soon became second nature.
And this, I think, Marcus clearly perceived beforehand.
Commodus was nineteen years old when his father died,
leaving him many guardians among whom were numbered the
best men of the Senate. But to their suggestions and counsels
Commodus soon said good-bye, and after making a truce with
the barbarians hastened to Rome, for he was a slacker, and
craved the ease of the City.

That is as good a *résumé* of Commodus' rise and fall as could ever
have been penned. Marcus had hoped to cure the boy's 'simplicity
and cowardice' by a kind of homoeopathic treatment: let him
share his father's burden, and so learn how honourable it was.
He was made a consul at the age of sixteen, younger than even
any prince before him. He was promoted to be co-regent younger
than any other prince, too. In Weber's words (CAH XI, p. 376):

> He assumed the *'cura rei publicae'* at the age at which Alexander
> entered on his inheritance, soon to add to it a conquered world;
> at which Caesar's adopted son began the conflict for his
> inheritance, to become Augustus and *pater patriae*. When
> Alexander, not yet thirty-three, lay on his deathbed, an epoch
> had been made in the history of the world; when the younger
> Caesar, not yet thirty-two, triumphed at Actium, his own
> strength had made sure his mastery of the Roman world;
> when Commodus, at a like age, gasped out his life in the
> clutch of an athlete, an opportunity of world-importance had
> been missed and what his predecessors had gathered, increased,
> guarded and sought to save had been lost.

There is no doubt that the plot against him which miscarried
deeply seared his unstable character: it was the *Senate* which had
sent him the fatal weapon. He must therefore regard that body
as his many-headed foe. He did. His wife Crispina, to whom he
had been married, under the stress of the Scythian war, sooner
than Marcus would otherwise have wished, was no help. She
had no influence on him, and as already related, was soon
banished and killed. Commodus' craven apprehensions, his
dislike of appearing in public, was naturally enough exploited by

his entourage, notably by Perennis the commander of the Guard. He "assumed all the cares of government—an arrangement which Commodus joyfully accepted". We can readily believe that, but that he kept a seraglio of three hundred girls and as many boys is open to question on physical no less than on moral grounds.

The only person who had any real hold on this disordered being was a woman called Marcia. She had been a concubine of Quadratus who was said to have conspired against Commodus and had been killed in 182. She was a remarkable woman. She had leanings towards Christianity, and showed favour to the Christians. She was soon the emperor's chief mistress, and behaved like an Augusta, and was treated like one, except that he was not allowed to be preceded by an attendant carrying fire, as a true empress would have been. "She was, in fact, the first great concubine in Roman history," as Balsdon terms her. She had Commodus in thrall. He loved to see her arrayed as an Amazon, and pictured as such. He even wanted to enter the arena dressed as an Amazon himself. He became more and more unhinged, and more and more homicidal; so that no-one felt safe, and very few were, especially those whose fortunes were worth appropriating. The senators trembled. Dio, who was a senator himself, thus describes an afternoon at the theatre, one of a celebration which lasted for fourteen successive days.

> When the emperor was fighting, we senators together with the knights always attended. Only Claudius Pompeianus the elder never appeared, but sent his sons, while remaining away himself; for he preferred even to be killed for this rather than to behold the emperor, the son of Marcus, conducting himself in such a fashion. For among other things that we did, we would shout out whatever we were commanded, and especially these words continually: 'Thou art lord and thou art first, of all men most fortunate. Victor thou art, and victor thou shalt be, from everlasting, Amazonian, thou art victor.' But of the populace in general many did not enter the amphitheatre at all, and others departed after merely glancing inside, partly from shame at what was going on, partly also from fear, inasmuch as a report spread abroad that he would want to shoot a few of the spectators in imitation of Hercules and the Stymphalian birds . . . This fear was shared by all, by us senators as well as by the rest. And here is another thing he

did to us senators which gave us every reason to look for our death. Having killed an ostrich and cut off its head, he came up to where we were sitting, holding the head in his left hand and in his right hand raising aloft his bloody sword; and though he spoke not a word, yet he wagged his head with a grin, indicating that he would treat us in the same way. And many of us would indeed have perished by the sword on the spot, for laughing at him (for it was laughter rather than indignation that overcame us), if I had not chewed some laurel leaves, which I got from my garland, myself, and persuaded the others who were sitting near to me to do the same, so that in the steady movement of our jaws we might conceal the fact that we were laughing.

At these exhibitions, Commodus claimed a fee of one million sesterces a day. He strutted and postured in his purple, gold-spangled robe, with a surcoat of the same hue, and a gold tiara glistening with Indian gems. The lion's skin and club of Hercules were exhibited on a gilded chair, even when he was not present. He would enter the lists bearing his herald's staff like that of Mercury. Then casting aside all this make-believe frippery, he would begin his exhibition clad only in a tunic and unshod.

Clearly so destructive a menace, maniac though he might be, could not last long. In fact he was soon despatched. But of the method of his execution, our sources are flimsy and in conflict. Dio, who is at pains to reassure us that he writes as a contemporary witness—"let no-one doubt this statement" he says—affirms that the mad emperor decided to give a spectacular exhibition of himself as all-vanquishing gladiator on New Year's Day, 193, possibly having killed the consuls; and with that end in view proposed to spend the preceding night in the gladiators' school, of which the vestiges have recently been brought to light, just east of the Colosseum. In fact he had booked a cell there, as if he were a common gladiator. When Commodus appeared in the amphitheatre, he was flanked by the prefect of the Guard, Aemilius Laetus, and his groom of the bedchamber, Eclectus. These two officers tried to dissuade their master from his shameful design. He answered them with threats. They therefore took Marcia into their confidence.

On the last day of the year, at night, when people were busy with the holiday, they caused Marcia to administer poison to him in some beef. But the immoderate use of wine and baths which was habitual with him, kept him from succumbing at once, and instead he vomited up some of it; and thus suspecting the truth, started uttering threats. They then sent Narcissus, an athlete, against him and caused this man to strangle him while he was taking a bath. Such was the end of Commodus, after he had ruled twelve years, nine months and fourteen days. He had lived thirty-one years and four months; and with him the line of the genuine Aurelii ceased to rule. [Only three sisters survived him.]

Nothing could be more precise, more circumstantial. How then can we account for the fact that Herodian, making Marcia the principal agent in the affair, repeats almost word for word the description which Dio has given (as hearsay) of the murder of Domitian, with the story of the little boy and the tablet and all? The answer is that we can do no such thing; even though the *Life* appears to give it some verisimilitude in Chapter IX: "He allowed statues of himself to be erected with the accoutrements of Hercules; and sacrifices were performed to him as to a god. He had planned to execute many more men besides, but his plan was betrayed by a certain young servant, who threw out of his bedroom a tablet on which were written the names of those who were to be killed." Where did the *Life* get that from? Herodian? We cannot tell. But we can tell from a passage in the *Life* of Avidius Cassius what sort of standards the author or authors of the collection regarded as allowable. Chapter II of that *Life* consists of an obviously spurious letter from Marcus to Verus. In it, first we have attributed to Pius (misnamed Verus' grandfather) a remark which Seneca made to Nero (p. 108 above); then a remark of Domitian's (p. 107) given to Hadrian, with this gloss: "I have preferred, moreover, to quote this as Hadrian's, rather than Domitian's who is reported to have said it first (Suetonius, *Domitian*, xxi), for good sayings when uttered by tyrants have not as much weight as they deserve." Which is another way of saying that any weight given to that *Life* (at any rate) is more than it could possibly deserve.

Marcia, at least, had acted with resolution. She and her associates kept their heads. After Commodus was dead, they approached a veteran of sixty-six named Pertinax. He was accepted by the army and the Senate, but after a blameless rule of three months he was murdered by the garrison. Poor Marcia and her two friends met their inevitable fate. But admiration and compassion must ever be our tribute to this queen of concubines.

Part III

CHAPTER X

'Politicke Dames'

THE ELEVATION AND fate of Pertinax stand as an ominous portent of what the future held for the empire. He was born the son of a seller of firewood in an obscure village of Liguria. He was tall, fair and handsome with naturally waving hair. His father gave him a good education. His own talents raised him to eminence. He was a personal friend of Dio, who gives a detailed account of his career. He was a competent soldier, and suppressed a dangerous revolt in Britain. He had simple tastes, and little ambition.

Marcus Aurelius, who realised his virtues, made him consul. Now that he was a prominent figure in Rome, he was able to make a brilliant marriage. His bride was Titiana, daughter of one of the richest members of the Senate. So popular was Pertinax that, when a horse of the same name won a race in the hippodrome, its success was greeted by the populace as a happy omen.

Neither Pertinax nor his wife were faithful spouses. Pertinax was bewitched by a lady called Cornificia. He was hardly troubled, therefore, when Titiana, growing weary of her now grey and paunchy mate, took up with a popular ballad-singer. She was, however, officially denied the title of Augusta, which nevertheless is accorded her on coins and in inscriptions.

Pertinax had many good qualities; but, as Dio puts it, he did not realise that "one cannot with safety reform everything at once and that the restoration of a state, in particular, requires both time and wisdom. He had lived sixty-seven years, lacking four months and three days, and had reigned eighty-seven days."

Poor Titiana. She had hopes that her father-in-law might

succeed her husband as emperor. That hope was soon to be dashed and, after her brief eminence, Titiana recedes into complete obscurity.

The murder of Pertinax seemed to have recreated the chaos of the year 98, the 'year of the four emperors'. The Praetorians mistakenly took that view. On the very evening of the murder, they put the purple up for auction. Hearing of the cynical commerce, a rich Milanese-born ex-consul called Julianus, egged on by his wife and daughter left the dinner-table 'in the midst of his cups and jollity', and hastened to the camp, where after spirited bidding against Titiana's father, he succeeded in getting the empire knocked down to him. The praetorians had miscalculated. This time the contest was not simply between rival candidates, but between competing armies and provinces. Julianus was arrogant and brutal. He is even said to have sacrificed children in obscene apotropaic rites. He lasted less than three months.

The Empire, in Herodian's phrase, now "hanged like a meteor in the sky and was exposed to him that could catch it". Three hands were outstretched for it, those of Albinus, in Britain, Niger in Syria, Septimius Severus in Pannonia. Niger was 'a dull Flegmatic'. Even if Herodian underestimates a little when he says "Rome is not very far from Britain", Severus knew that Pannonia was nearer. He temporised with Albinus, and so won the race for Rome. Severus was Punic, his wife Julia Domna, Syrian. Both were Semites. "Julia, wife of Severus, was one of the empresses who made most noise in the world. Her high position, gallantries, love of knowledge, and esteem for learned men, her troubles and even her death, have made her name famous in history." Thus does Molesworth introduce the empress Julia Domna. If we except the world 'gallantries' it is a balanced resumé of Julia's character and career—we must remember that Molesworth was translating an eighteenth century Frenchman, for whom 'gallantries' were a basic ingredient of any woman. In fact, Julia made more 'noise in the world' than Molesworth allows her. Balsdon sums her up succinctly and accurately.

Julia's round face and Syrian features did not constitute beauty of the first order; but she had great intelligence and great courage, and her influence and personality pervaded the whole empire. The record of no other empress survives in so many inscriptions and on so many coins. She was a more powerful figures even than Plotina, and was the most powerful empress that Rome had yet experienced.

Or would experience. Livia's grandeur had helped to establish the Empire, Plotina's prudence had assisted its consolidation. Julia Domna's breadth of outlook and determination as exercised by herself and her family were not only to be paramount until the middle of the third century; but she, her sister and her two nieces were endowed with a potency that was to elevate mono-theism to become the most favoured cult in the whole empire. These four ladies were indeed what our English Herodian calls them—'politicke dames'. Unlike any of their predecessors they were not content to maintain the imperial fabric, they transformed it. They inherited the mildewed aftermath of an old empire: they sowed the vigorous seeds of a new one.

To form some idea of the deep and lasting influence which the emperor and his Augusta were to exercise on the Roman world, let us try to grasp their environment, to chart in some measure the currents amid which they were first launched into the world. Husband and wife came from opposite ends of the Empire, he from the west, she from the east. The backgrounds of both were equally exotic. Never before had Rome acquired rulers so un-Roman. Trajan and Hadrian had hailed from Spain, the Antonines from Provence. They brought with them to Italy the ampler outlook of the lands of their birth; but they were all of Italian, of Roman stock; their minds moved along Roman lines. Those of the new sovereigns did not. They might be Romanised—he far more than she—but they never lost the feeling of being alien. Severus tried to exorcise it by what we might now call over-compensation: he would be more imperious than any previous emperor. Julia being a woman simply disregarded it. Only the sons would show it, disastrously.

When we come to this juncture in Roman affairs, we feel more than ever how unsatisfactory are our literary sources. The *Augustan History* is as usual unreliable. Dio is ambivalent. As a Bithynian Greek, or Greek-speaker, he had little sympathy for what he regarded as Semitic intruders; at the same time, he had been a consul with Julia's great-nephew, Alexander Severus, when Alexander was emperor. He has already told us that he was reporting events from his own knowledge; but when he comes

to the latter end of this fascinating dynasty, he hedges. He writes:
"Thus far"—that is up to the year 222 when Alexander became
emperor—

> I have described events with as great accuracy as I could in
> every case, but for subsequent events I have not found it
> possible to give an accurate account, for the reason that I did
> not spend much time in Rome. For after going from Asia to
> Bithynia, I fell sick, and from there I hastened to my province
> of Africa; then on returning to Italy I was almost immediately
> sent as governor first to Dalmatia and then to Upper Pannonia,
> and though after that I returned to Rome and Campania, I at
> once set out for home [Nicaea]. For these reasons I have not
> been able to compile the same sort of account of subsequent
> events as of the earlier ones.

Later he tells us that when in Italy he preferred Campania to
Rome, at the emperor's urging, for reasons of security; but left
as soon as he could for home, because of his gout. Poor excuses,
these: as Caesar's friend Dio was better placed than any man
living to know just what was going on all over the empire and
why. We feel justified in resenting his reticence.

Herodian again, being a Greek or Hellenised Syrian, is apt to
be a bit 'superior' when writing about a 'native', however exalted
(and so a target for jealousy) Julia had become. He tells us at the
outset of his history that it is founded upon 'no vulgar aires or
vaine noises', but on true relations. He despises the 'heart-
burning and spightful emulation of the Greeks', such people as
'win and wedge men to their several factions'. It was of the
Greeks of Alexandria he was thinking, a 'cock-brained and light-
headed lot'. Herodian is as tantalising as Dio. He might have
told us so much more, instead of boring us with those dreary
speeches. But in the general dearth of fact, Herodian is valuable.
"*Dans le royaume des aveugles le borgnis est roi.*" And while he says
almost nothing about Julia, he does give us one almost Racinian
glimpse of her misery.

Fortunately we have two other sources of information—
archaeology and the brilliant researches of modern scholars.

Septimius was a native of Lepcis Magna, in northern Africa,
having been born there on 11th April 146. His ancestors had been
made knights, two of his great-uncles had been consuls.

Lepcis Magna was a splendid and prosperous city. By the end of the second century BC, it had become like many another peripheral metropolis, the 'friend and ally' of the Roman people—the usual preliminary to absorption by Rome, which in the case of Lepcis occurred in the year 47 BC, when Julius Caesar reduced the town to 'stipendiary', that is subordinate, status. The genius of Roman rule at its best was that when it demanded tribute in cash or kind it also produced the conditions on which that tribute could be provided. Lepcis throve; joined with two other cities, Oea (modern Tripoli) and Sabratha, it gave the region the name of Tripolitania, the land of three cities. Three times towards the end of the first century AD marauders from the southern desert were repelled. The cities were rewarded by being made 'colonies' that is they acquired Roman citizenship, which in the provinces was still a coveted honour. Lepcis was thus elevated in the year 109, under Trajan, and was styled 'the faithful'—*Colonia Ulpia Traiana Fidelis Lepcis Magna*.

The city, or what is left of it, astonishes by its size. It covers more than 300 acres, about the area of the state of Monaco. And what profusion! There are streets, triumphal arches, porticoes, temples, forums, baths, gymnasium, basilica, theatre, amphitheatre, a stone barrage athwart a stream-bed to ensure a copious water-supply, and a commodious harbour, complete with bollarded quays and a lighthouse. For the people who built and dwelt in this great city were a maritime folk. They lived and laboured between the desert and the deep sea, on which they fared far and wide, east and west, as merchants. The olive-groves that furnished them with much of their wealth are a mere break between the city and the desert. It was to the sea that they looked for a living. The city is built on the shore, almost on the beach itself, like Tyre or Sidon, or Salamis in Cyprus, and for the same reason.

When we examine the monuments, we observe that although in their architecture they conform to, or adopt, Graeco-Roman models, the inscriptions on them are carved not only in Latin, but in another, unfamiliar script. It is neo-Punic. Many of the names, too, are reminiscent of the days of Hannibal. Annobal Rufus gave the theatre and the market, and his munificence is recorded both in Latin and in Punic. Another bilingual inscription proclaims that G'y ben Hanno embellished a colonnade. The decoration itself is reminiscent of the east, of Syria and Mesopotamia, both in the themes employed—the vine, for instance

which figured in Herod's Temple and is still admired in its
successor, the Dome of the Rock—and in the intricacy of its
execution, quite alien to the straightforward Roman work. This
is particularly true, significantly enough, of the portion of the
town which arose under the patronage of its most famous son
Septimius Severus. Surveying Lepcis and its wonders we are
bound to concede that Carthage, which was officially deemed to
have ceased to exist in 146 BC, was still very much alive. How
tough, agile and enduring these Semites were. Originally traders
from Phoenicia, they were content at first, these merchants, to
make periodical voyages, to traffic for slaves, gold and the ivory
which came from the deep south of Africa. Gradually the trading-
posts became settlements. The greatest of them was called
Carthage, the New City. Carthage and Rome first encountered
each other as wary rivals, bound by a treaty of 507 BC, which
recognised the pre-emptive right of Carthage to conduct the
carrying trade. The inevitable clash came in 264. It took Rome
more than a century to humble Carthage. Carthage was destroyed
in 146 BC, but the Carthaginians were not. Dido queen of
Carthage is represented in Virgil's *Aeneid*, not as a forlorn woman,
but as an imperial menace. Aeneas, in forsaking her is but doing
his Roman duty. Cleopatra was regarded as a second Dido,
Berenice as a third. *Punica Fides*, Punic Faith, meaning the lack
of it, treachery in fact—how could a man born of such ancestry
be received as the loyal servant of Rome, let alone as its master?
    Severus it is true, took pains to learn both Latin and Greek,
both of which languages he spoke with a Punic accent, but they
spoke Punic in the family, and when his sister and nephew visited
him after he became emperor, he was so ashamed of them that
they were hastily loaded with presents and bundled back home.
Basically, Severus, too, remained a Semite, proud of his ancestry
and culture, so much older and deeper-rooted than that of Rome.
    Severus' rise to eminence is as mysterious as it was rapid. If
only we possessed his autobiography, even if as Dio hints (LXXVI,
7, 3) it was not wholly trustworthy. But Dio is often ungratefully
patronising towards his one-time benefactor. From childhood
Septimius seems to have been determined to shine. Although of
less than normal stature—here the representation of him on the
moneychangers' arch in Rome, which shows him shorter than
Julia, confirms Dio—he was well-built, handsome and command-
ing. Mentally he was keen and vigorous. "As for education,"

a) Empress Julia Domna, the wife of Septimius Severus and niece of Julia Mammaea

b) Julia Mammaea, mother of Severus Alexander

c) Julia Moesa

d) The Black Stone being conveyed to Rome, as shown on a coin in the Bibliothèque Nationale. The inscription reads SANCT DEO SOLI—'to the holy god the sun', and below ELAGABAL

Julia Mammaea, a head now in the Terme National Museum, Rome

adds Dio (LXXVII, 16, 1), "he was eager for more than he obtained, and for this reason was a man of few words though of many ideas. When he was eighteen or soon after he came to Rome to pursue his studies, and," we are surprised to read, "with the support of his kinsman Septimius Severus, who had already been consul twice, he sought and secured from the deified Marcus the broad stripe", that is, the young man from Lepcis was granted senatorial status. He modelled himself, not unnaturally as being an 'outlander', on Hadrian, and like Hadrian he prospered. After serving as quaestor in Rome, he went in the same capacity to Baetica, the very province from which Hadrian had sprung. He crossed to Africa to settle his domestic affairs after the death of his father, and while there was transferred to Sardinia. He was then about twenty-five. Next, we find him proconsul of Africa. He made it quite clear that this was no mere return of the native, but the advent of an imperial governor: an over-exuberant old comrade who embraced him while on parade was soundly beaten, and proclamation made that "No plebeian may embrace a legate of the Roman People".

Marcus Aurelius appointed him tribune of the people, and praetor, at the age of thirty-two. He had already married his first wife, Marcia, of whom we know nothing except that he made no mention of her in his autobiography, but erected statues to her memory when he became emperor. Marcia died before he was forty.

While serving in the other northern Spanish province, he was commanded in a dream to repair the temple of Augustus at the capital Tarraco—just as Hadrian had done. To Septimius who, even by contemporary standards, was abnormally superstitious, the inference was clear. It was fortified by a second dream of even more direct import.

After military service in Syria he visited Athens, whose citizens did not take to this enquiring Semite, any more than they had to an earlier one, Paul of Tarsus. The vindictive African had his own back on them when he became emperor.

At the age of forty-five, or perhaps a little earlier, we find the handsome and highly eligible widower (for Commodus had continued his father's patronage of Severus) as governor of southern Gaul, of which the capital was Lugdunum (Lyons). It was here that he decided to marry again. A man so high in official favour could have allied himself with one of the first families of

Rome. Instead Severus decided to marry the daughter of a Syrian prince-priest. In Balsdon's words (p. 151):

> He happily remembered at Lyons in his Residence as Governor of the province of Gallia Lugdunensis, that when he had done service in Syria, commanding the legion IV, he had visited the temple of the Sun [Elagabal] at Emesa, made the acquaintance of Julius Bassianus the priest, who as his office showed, was a man of breeding, and of his daughter Julia Domna. Either then or later he had learnt that she had a horoscope which matched the promise of his own dreams. She was destined to be a ruler's wife. So he sent for her and married her. This in 185.

If ever there was a 'dynastic marriage' it was this. It is easy to imagine the profound effect which Syria must have had on Septimius. Here, a thousand miles from his homeland, he entered a society which was familiar, which spoke his own language, which was indeed the cradle of his race. What a discovery—and what a release. No need here to pretend to be more Roman than Rome. He humbled the saucy Greeks of Antioch: he would now exalt his cousin-Semites. And how more definitely and obviously than by marrying one; a very prominent lady, too. To Julia Domna, as to her relations, the prospect of her rising to be empress was alluring enough. "Through the mediation of his friends"—that would be essential in the Levant—he secured his bride.

Julia came from Emesa, the modern Homs, a town which dominates the plain, tawny and fertile in contrast to the pallid grit of the desert which lies to the east and south of it. Through this plain flows the infant Orontes, pausing on the way to nourish the lake which in antiquity as now formed the reservoir of an elaborate irrigation system. The chief importance of Homs however was, and still is, that it forms a staging-post between Palmyra to the east and the gap in the mountain chain which gives access to the Phoenician littoral. Its material prosperity in antiquity fluctuated, as the late Henri Seyrig pointed out, with that of Palmyra. Today one may meet in Homs the most mixed yet least cosmopolitan throng in all Syria; for it is still the meeting-place of tribesman and townsman, of farmer and nomad, of all the multitudinous types that constitute the population of

Syria. The railway-junction and the oil refinery seem extra-
territorial, irrelevant. Emesa of old had something of the same
quality: it was in the Roman province of Syria, but not of it.
It led its own cultural life, and to what exquisite heights its arts
were raised may be gauged from the silver helmet, the rings, gold
ornaments and seals, preserved in the Damascus Museum.

But the eminence of Emesa was due primarily to religion.
Syria, including the Lebanon, has always been the most prolific
parent, or ardent foster-parent of religions. It still harbours a
remarkable variety of them. Within the boundaries of this single
region, little more than 200 miles square, are to be found Muslims,
both Sunni and Shi'a, Druses, Alaouites, Jews, Orthodox
Christians, Maronites, Armenians, both Orthodox and Uniate,
Roman Catholics, Greek Catholics, Syrians, Nestorians, Chaldeans, Anglicans, Quakers and Seventh Day Adventists. The
Syrian, Chaldean and Nestorian Churches still use Aramaic as
their liturgical language. In certain villages near Damascus,
Aramaic, the language in which Jesus and his disciples spoke with
each other, is still the vernacular.

In Julia's day there were many holy cities in Syria, none holier
than Emesa. Emesa was ruled by a dynasty of prince-priests
dedicated to the service of the sun-god. In truth the setting is
apt for such a cult, because the acropolis of Homs, a rocky out-
crop from the plain, stands up in the light of day like the gnomon
of a sundial.

The princes of Emesa first enter Roman history in the days of
Pompey in 64 BC, and the entry they make is dignified and
important. The then ruling prince was called Sampsigeramus, a
name meaning probably "The Sun hath established"—the first
syllable is certainly the Semitic *shams*, meaning sun. Pompey
became such friends with him that Cicero, in writing to his
friend Atticus, more than once calls Pompey 'Sampsigeramus',
hoping that the courier would not know to whom he was referring.

The dynasty continued in authority and prestige under Roman
protection. In AD 44 King Agrippa I of Judaea, when he summoned a conference of kings at his new capital of Tiberias,
included the prince of Emesa, a later Sampsigeramus, among
the guests. His brother Aristoboulos had in fact married the
daughter of an earlier prince, called Suheim. In 52 Agrippa's own
daughter Drusilla married the ruler of Emesa, 'Aziz. These
alliances between the Herods and the ruling family of Emesa are

doubly significant: they show that the Herods, who were very proud of being royal, regarded the Emesans as being 'good enough', and also that they could make some claim however vague, to be regarded as 'monotheists' in their capacity as Sun-worshippers—a fact which was later to emerge into the first political importance.

To say therefore, as some did, that Julia Domna's origin was lowly or obscure was the reverse of true. She came from an ancient and regal family, of high religious prestige, which had been on familiar terms with Rome for two hundred years.

This was perfectly well known and acknowledged at the Roman court. The wedding was celebrated in the temple of Venus 'near the Palace', and one of the imperial ladies herself prepared the marriage chamber, which shows that the union had official blessing.

The family continued to rule, as we know from inscriptions: it was still ruling in Emesa after it had ceased to rule in Rome. Before that happened, it was to give Rome an empress, who was to be the mother of two others and the great-aunt of yet two more.

Septimius and his wife swept onward. From the business point of view, she was the ideal partner. She had been brought up to be a princess, educated in every quirk of intrigue and policy. She was equally at home in the closet or the camp. She was, as even her detractors had to admit, of a nimble wit and ready device 'as the Syrians generally are'. Septimius proved a popular governor of Gaul, and later administered Pannonia and Sicily. Julia realised that Commodus, despite the favour he had shown them, could not last long. She was prepared for the great opportunity. Septimius was commander-in-chief in Pannonia when Commodus was killed.

Septimius made for Rome by forced marches. His troops slept in their armour. The speed of his advance paralysed opposition. He entered the vital fortress of Ravenna unopposed. He pressed on to Rome. He found the city in confusion. The Praetorians were utterly demoralised by soft living, the marines from Misenum had forgotten how to drill. Even the elephants mutinied, throwing their 'castles' and riders.

Septimius made a triumphal entry into Rome. It was the most magnificent spectacle Dio had ever beheld, as he moved arrayed in his state robes among the rejoicing populace, through streets bright with flowers and tapestries and fragrant with the perfumes of Arabia.

The praetorian Guard had already been disbanded by a stratagem they of all men should have seen through—a fake invitation to a victory celebration with laurels in place of arms: that they did not shows how astute and artful Septimius was. They were replaced by a new body of troops drawn from all legions alike. Formerly only men from Italy, Spain, Noricum (Austria) and Macedonia had been eligible. Dio blamed Severus for this: the old guard were more respectable in habit and manners; the new recruits were a motley throng of savages, he complains. Niger and Albinus were both liquidated.

The new emperor had been tactful enough to enter Rome in civilian attire. He held a grand memorial service for Pertinax, whose avenger he claimed to be. He even took the name Pertinax, but soon discarded it in favour of a name of happier augury. He announced that he had been adopted into the Antonine family, and hailed Commodus as his 'brother'. This was not quite so ridiculous as it might sound. Both Marcus and Commodus had shown him marked favour as a young man, as had at least one Palace lady. (Dio or his epitomiser says it was the younger Faustina 'wife of Marcus' who had been matron of honour at his wedding; but Faustina had died nine years earlier: it may have been Vitrasia Faustina, afterwards killed by Commodus.) If Hadrian, whom Septimius had taken as his model, had been adopted only on the deathbed of his predecessor, might not Septimius carry the principle just one stage further back, and assume a posthumous adoption?

Thus was the empire transformed. Technically, an Antonine, approved by the Senate, now ruled Rome. In fact it was a Semite of the west, allied to a Semite of the east, both of them brilliant manipulators of a régime founded on armed authority, who now dominated the empire. A new star had arisen, and it was from the east that it shone.

Naturally enough, Julia Domna was charmed with Rome. She felt quite at home there: after all, her family had been 'Roman' far longer than her husband's. Besides it was comforting to see how firmly, how augustly, the cult of the Sun was already established in the capital. Its oldest, most venerable, embellishments were those obelisks, those 'gifts to the Sun' which Augustus and his successors had imported or imitated. But in the early part of the reign, Julia was to see little of Rome. *"Ubi imperator, ibi Roma"*—"where the emperor is, there is Rome," a courtier had said to Commodus. Septimius proved it true. In the first ten years of his reign, he visited Rome only on three flying visits, in 193 (the year of his accession), in 196 and 197, amounting to less than a twelvemonth in all. It was the east which had chiefly claimed him.

"The remote nations of the Levant," says Herodian, "so far disjoined by sea and land, scarce bear the name of Italy." They were now to hear it very clearly, and, in general, to their advantage.

The statement above that Niger and Albinus had been liquidated covers two civil wars of a destructive savagery such as Rome had not seen since the last days of the republic. Niger must first be suppressed lest he seize Egypt, as Vespasian had done, and so hold Rome to ransom. Severus directed the campaign from Perinthus, on the sea of Marmara. Niger made Antioch his headquarters. Forced back through the Cicilian Gates (Gülek Boghaz) he was finally defeated at Issus on the battlefield where Alexander the Great had defeated Darius in 330 BC. Niger left 20,000 dead behind him as he fled for Antioch. He was soon caught and killed. Only Byzantium still defied Severus. The victor ordered Niger's head to be paraded outside the walls. To no effect: Byzantium held out for another two years.

Severus entered Antioch in triumph. Like Hadrian before him, Severus had good reason to dislike the Antiochenes who had treated 'the African' with disdain when he had been their over-lord in the days of Marcus Aurelius. Severus now did what Hadrian had considered doing: he divided Syria into two, in order to reduce the power of its governor and to humble the arrogance of these sneering pseudo-Hellenes. Coele-Syria, or Hollow Syria, was to consist of the northern half of the former province with Commagene added, and Laodicea (Lataqia) was to replace Antioch as its capital. Phoenician Syria was to comprise the south as far as the borders of Judaea. Tyre and Damascus already enjoyed the status of metropolis.

After a brief visit to Rome, he hurried north for what he knew would be the decisive battle of his career. Hitherto he had never taken the field in person: now he knew he must do so. At the battle of Lyons on the 19th February 197, Albinus was routed. He committed suicide, and Severus sent his head to the Senate as a present. He now divided Britain into two as he had divided

Syria, and for the same reason. When he reached Rome in June, he executed twenty-nine senators—on his accession he had vowed to execute none—who had supported Albinus: and confiscated their estates. He needed the money, to bribe the citizens and to cajole the soldiers, who were besides at last allowed to contract legal marriages while on active service, and senior NCO's and centurions were granted the privilege of wearing the gold ring which had previously been the insignia of knights.

The Senate were shown what their relative position was by being forced to confirm the army's proclamation of Caracalla as Caesar in place of Albinus, and the deification of Commodus. Severus had already told them that he intended to model himself on the severity of Marcus, Sulla and Augustus.

No shred of the 'republican' shroud in which for two centuries the body politic had lain embalmed now remained. In two decades a purportedly 'civil' government had been replaced by a bold brazen military dictatorship, and it was a bold, brazen African, brilliantly seconded by a subtle Syrian, who had done it.

Severus was now determined to call the old world into existence to restore the balance of the new: for almost the next five years, 'Rome' was to be in Syria and Egypt. It was the sovereigns' intention to make the region of Julia's origin more brilliant than ever. But first the clever African realised that for home consumption what was needed was a resounding military victory over the hereditary foe, Parthia. This was duly achieved, and the greedy soldiery were indulged by being suffered to loot the Parthian capital, Ctesiphon. Severus had made good the boast which Dio says he uttered three years earlier after the campaign against Niger, that he had created a strong bulwark on the Euphrates frontier of Syria. What he did not realise was that by humbling the Parthians he was preparing the way for the far more formidable Persian Sassanids, who at no distant date would humiliate Rome.

Back in the Levant, Septimius and his wife proceeded to elevate the already opulent province to an unprecedented zenith of prosperity and magnificence, of which the vestiges even after the devastations of eighteen hundred years, the ravages of war, rapine and earthquakes still astound us. Ba'albek, city of the Sun, granted Italian status, saw its sanctuary embellished with giant granite monoliths from Egypt, hauled up 3,850 feet above the level of the sea; Palmyra too was adorned and granted the status of a colony with the name 'Septimian'. Jerash, which in its western baths exhibits the epoch-making new invention of a dome on pendentives (that is, a circular vault on a square building, contrived as an intrinsic member of the structure) which was to transform architectural achievement; Samaria in Palestine— these are but four of the cities which throughout the area were to benefit from the exuberant renaissance wrought by Severus at his wife's behest. Unfortunately, in Abel's words, the emperor influenced by his wife, continued to "gather grapes after the vintage", that is to pursue personal enmities. Antioch, for instance, had to wait a year and a half before its ancient rights were restored. But in general the benefits far outweighed the wounds. Ulpian, the eminent jurist who was a member of Septimius' privy council, and himself a Tyrian, lauds his master's generosity as follows:

It should be known that there are colonies which enjoy Italian rights, such as the most splendid colony of the Tyrians, of which I am a native . . . of great antiquity, strongly fortified, very faithful to the alliance which it has concluded with the Romans, on which in fact the deified Severus our emperor bestowed Italian rights because of its outstanding loyalty to the Roman republic and empire.

After a vist to Palestine and Egypt, the imperial suite spent the winter at Antioch, and it was here that on the first day of the year 202 that Septimius assumed his third consulate with Caracalla as his colleague. The lad was now sixteen, had adopted the name Antoninus, and had already, at the age of eleven been proclaimed Augustus by the army (what did the Senate matter, here in the east?) the title Caesar being transferred to Geta his brother. The Senate had decreed him a triumph at the age of twelve! Such fawning complaisance might have undermined a stronger and less susceptible character than that of the precociously psychopathic Caracalla.

After inspecting the eastern section of the northern frontier, and the new married quarters in the garrison towns, Septimius reached Rome in time to celebrate, from 2nd to 8th June, his *decennalia*, the tenth anniversary of his reign, after an absence from his capital of almost five years. The proceedings were impressive, but not on so grand a scale as those which marked Severus' first entry into Rome ten years before. For one thing, he was suffering so severely from gout that he was unable to stand in a chariot, so that there was no formal triumph. No one had cause to complain: every citizen on the free corn register and every member of the Guard was given ten gold pieces, one for each year of the reign. As a permanent record of the event a splendid building-programme was undertaken. The fire of 192, the last year of Commodus' reign, had ravaged a large part of Rome, including the Forum and the Palatine. Only now, eleven years later, in a Rome victorious and at peace, could the task of restoration be tackled. Before the old was renewed, there was one new personal addition to be made to the Roman scene, a triumphal arch. Cramped and cluttered though the Forum had now become, room must be made within its boundaries for Septimius' memorial, because he planned to revive, in the year 204, the Secular Games, and through his own arch the sacred band of lads and virgins, chanting their hallowed hymns must pass. These exercises had been founded in 509 BC, and under the early Republic had been celebrated at intervals averaging about a century, whence their name. Augustus had revived them in 17 BC, and had commissioned Horace to write his *Carmen Seculare* for the occasion. Claudius, Domitian and above all Antoninus had resuscitated them. The new Antoninus must do the same.

The arch, which with disdainful bravura stands within fifty paces of the senate-house, is an eloquent exposition of the character and achievements of him who ordained it. It is a family monument, recording the victories of the father and two sons (though here as throughout the Empire the name of Geta was later replaced by other words), who "restored the commonwealth and promoted the rule of the Roman people by their outstanding merit both at home and abroad". They had, too. Septimius himself, so run the farcéd titles, is hailed as *Pontifex Maximus, Father of the Fatherland*, four times *Imperator*, holder of the *Tribunician Authority, Parthicus Arabicus, Parthicus Adiabenicus* (Adiabene was in northern Mesopotamia). The sculpture of the arch, though the style shows signs of decline from Antonine grace, illustrates and corroborates these ascriptions.

On the contemporary Arch of the Money-changers in the Forum Boarium, Julia is not only represented as a co-celebrant with Septimius at an official sacrifice, but reaps her harvest of titles as well. Already in 196, after Septimius' defeat of the Adiabeni, she had been dubbed 'Mother of the Army', as the younger Faustina had been. Now she is hailed as 'Mother of the Augusti'—Caracalla and Geta—'and of the Army.' When the inscription was revised after Geta's death, she becomes 'Mother of our Augustus'—Caracalla—'and of the Army and of the Senate and the Country'. It is the army that, significantly enough, comes first. Septimius repaired the Portico of Octavia, near the theatre of Marcellus, and the Pantheon, which still bears his name. Julia made her showing, too. She restored the Temple of Vesta, a pretty little feminine rotunda in the very middle of the Forum, and the house of the Vestals which adjoins it at the foot of the Palatine. It seems rather large for the six ladies who inhabited it, but we must remember that it was also the repository of wills and testaments, the Somerset House of Rome.

Septimius' greatest—and most conspicuous—works were on the Palatine, and in the region to the south of it. Facing the Appian Way, he built what was called the Septizonium, or Septizodium. This was apparently a three-storeyed building, like a nymphaeum and probably modelled on the nymphaeum at Lepcis, because its object was to remind wayfarers from Africa, who would enter the City from that side, of the glories of their native land, now installed here in Rome, a sure psychological touch. We have early engravings of the structure, and it is represented in one of Botticelli's frescoes in the Sistine Chapel; but the last traces of it were demolished by Pope Sixtus V in 1588-9.

As the Palace itself had been so badly gutted by the fire of 192, Septimius and Julia planned a magnificent new wing, at the south extremity. It was to be even more remote from the busy Forum than Domitian's palace. To this end, the emperor erected a series of buildings supported on brick substructures, which for audacity and grace cannot be surpassed. The new buildings included a bath, for which water was conveyed through a branch of the Aqua Claudia, spanning the valley between the Palatine and the Caelian hills at an altitude which recalls the aqueduct of Segovia. It may well have been at this time that the lovely nymphaea on the hill were given their strikingly oriental aspect and function. The sunken hippodrome, or a predecessor, may have been included in the general design. Finally to the south arose the great Antonine Baths, a vast complex of which the ruins remain one of the most impressive relics in the whole range of Roman antiquity. These baths were started by Septimius and finished by Caracalla, by whose name they are popularly known. It was from the ruins of these baths that many of the finest pieces in the Farnese collection, including the famous bull now in the Naples Museum, were recovered. It was in these same ruins that Shelley wrote the greater part of *Prometheus Unbound*.

To commemorate this renovation of Rome, Septimius had a map of it engraved on marble, 18 metres wide and 20 high, the scale being 1:250. At various dates since 1562 fragments of it have come to light. They are now preserved in the Capitoline Museum, and have a curiously precise and modern "Survey" look.

Well might the imperial couple gaze out over the reborn City, and reflect with satisfaction upon the apogee of power and glory to which Fate had elevated them. But not for long. The year 202 marked their zenith.

As part of the *decennalia* celebrations, Septimius had arranged that his son Caracalla should marry. He could have selected any of the daughters of the Roman nobility, but he did not. In fact the choice was not his at all, and it certainly was not Julia's, nor even Caracalla's. The choice was that of an evil man, and it was the fruit of blackmail. Plautianus was a fellow-countryman of Severus. He was also a relation and in his youth, Herodian tells us, had been his bed-mate. As Severus rose in the world, Plautianus blackmailed his way up with him. By exploiting that shameful memory, by holding over the head of Severus the perpetual menace of exposure, he established an arrogant ascendancy over him. He regarded himself as the equal of the emperor: others regarded him as the emperor's superior. Once for instance when Plautianus was ill and Septimius called to enquire, the sick man's bodyguard arrogantly forbade his suite to enter. On another occasion when Severus wanted to judge a court case, the usher refused to call it, saying: "I dare not do so without orders from Plautianus." This vile man had contrived to have himself made not only sole, but perpetual prefect of the Guard. In Dio's words, "he wanted everything, asked everything from everybody, and would take everything." He sent for zebras from Somalia, sacred to the sun. He regarded himself as the sun of Rome, whom it was sacrilege even to behold: men must avert their gaze as he strutted through the streets, preceded by a throng of attendants. He was notoriously unchaste both with women and boys; but to preserve the chastity of his daughter he castrated a hundred noble Romans, not only boys, but married men as well. His wife he kept in strict purdah: not even the empress might see her. Not that Julia would have wished to. Naturally enough she abhorred Plautianus, who retaliated by impugning her honour, and before the very emperor himself. Julia in despair and disgust found solace in her philosophic study-circle.

Severus did at one stage rid himself of this incubus; but not for long, and woe betide those who had dared to assume that he was done for! They were soon murdered, even so prominent a citizen as a governor of Sardinia.

To crown his insolence Plautianus decided that having usurped the authority and status of one emperor, he would become the father-in-law of the next: Caracalla should marry his daughter Plautilla. Severus, Julia, Carcalla himself were all violently opposed to the match; but Plautianus had his way, and they were duly joined in a travesty of matrimony. Plautilla, despite her sheltered upbringing was besides being ill-bred, vicious and dissolute. To make the breach between Caracalla and his father-in-law irremediable, in the following year (203) Plautianus became consul, with Geta, Caracalla's brother, whom he loathed, as his colleague. This was too much. For one thing it was still regarded as improper that the same man should be both prefect and senator (though there were precedents and the dual honour was later legalised by Severus Alexander); for another, although Severus had bestowed the consular insignia on Plautianus he had never held the office, and so should now have been grateful for his first consulship, instead of which he flaunted his second. With his brother as it were gone over to the enemy, Caracalla felt isolated. Besides, his father-in-law was acting as a censor, prying into the rather dingy personal affairs of the young Augustus.

Caracalla decided to get rid of him. Plautianus imagined that he was invulnerable, and so thought nothing was amiss when he was summoned to the Palace alone and at night. Septimius had been primed to believe that Plautianus had been plotting against him. When he reproached Plautianus the prefect was taken aback, whereupon Caracalla struck him with his fist, and then disregarding his father ordered one of the bodyguard to kill him then and there. Someone plucked a few hairs from his beard and carried them to Julia and Plautilla, who, realising that something untoward was afoot, were waiting in an adjacent chamber. "Here's your Plautianus," he cried, to the horror of one and the relief of the other. The next day, January 23rd 205. Septimius addressed the Senate, merely blaming himself for being over-indulgent to the dead man. His wife and her brother were saved by being banished to the Lipari islands: a brief respite—they were soon killed. So vast were Plautianus' ill-gotten gains that a special commissioner was appointed to administer them.

Sadly, in the year 208, the ailing emperor set out on what he knew would be his last journey. It took him to Britain. His wife and sons accompanied him. While they were in Scotland (where Severus was able to verify Ptolemy's calculation of the solar parallax) Julia met a highland lady, in conversation with whom she criticised the Scottish liking for promiscuous sexual relations. Whereupon the Caledonian retorted: "In satisfying the needs of nature, our behaviour is a good deal better than yours. We pick up the best men and consort with them openly. At Rome you choose the worst and let them have you in secret." Queen Victoria would have approved this rebuke. It is the kind of remark that Brown might have made to a self-righteous Sassenach.

Septimius Severus died at York on the 4th February, 211, in the sixty-fifth year of his age, "not without help, they say, from Antoninus [Caracalla]". On his death-bed he had admonished his two sons: "Agree: enrich the soldiers: despise all the rest." For Julia the journey back to Rome, with her husband's ashes, and her warring children was a penance. Caracalla was now unhinged mentally. With no-one, neither father nor father-in-law to check them, both he and Geta indulged in every form of sexual licence. Caracalla went further: he was convinced, ever since his visit to Egypt with his parents, during which the party had beheld the tomb of Alexander, that he, Caracalla, was the new Alexander; and in his statues he adopted the hero's stance, with the head half turned to the left, to which he added a brutish scowl in place of the bland benignity of his model. He was determined to kill Geta, and kill him he did. At first he had a vague plan for dividing the empire between his brother and himself. Julia vetoed it: "But how will you divide your mother?" she said. So murder must be the Only Way. Pretending that he desired a reconciliation, he enticed Geta into his mother's chamber, and then slaughtered him in her arms. What is more, he insisted that Julia pretend to be glad that her precious Caracalla had been saved from assassination, and to give thanks for it, instead of being allowed to mourn.

But Julia was indomitable. Caracalla was to survive and rule for six years. His reign is memorable for the act whereby in 212 he made all free inhabitants of the empire Roman citizens. This is generally regarded, as Dio was the first to claim, as a method of increasing the revenue, as aliens were exempt from taxes and citizens were not. But we may also see in it another example of Caracalla's anti-Roman bias, at which Dio also seems to hint when he says that he possessed the vices of three races—"the fickleness, cowardice, and recklessness of the Gauls [he was born at Lyons], the harshness and cruelty of Africa [his father's homeland] and the craftiness of Syria whence he was sprung on his mother's side".

Julia found consolation in philosophy and literature. Dio was one of her *protégés*, and it was ungenerous of him, as well as inaccurate, to describe her as of 'demonic' birth. Philostratus, author of the *Lives of the Sophists*, was her secretary. She commissioned from him a still extant 'life' of Apollonius of Tyana, a thaumaturge who flourished under Domitian. He wrote letters to Julia, and styled her Julia the philospher.

And yet in a curious, warped sort of way, Caracalla trusted his mother, and it was that very trust that was to lead to his death. In the year 214-15 Caracalla was campaigning in the east, against the Parthians and Armenians. Julia was in Bithynia. So great was his reliance on Julia, that he made her his secretary-general, and empowered her to deal with all official correspondence. His despatches to the Senate were sent in her name as well as in the name of himself and the army.

In 217, Julia had moved to Antioch. While there, she received a letter addressed to her son, warning him that a Moorish officer called Macrinus, now a praetorian prefect and on Caracalla's staff, was determined to kill him. Before this letter could be delivered to Caracalla, Macrinus had received one from a friend in Rome, from which he realised that he must act at once. As on 6th April 217, Caracalla's birthday, the emperor was on his way to the temple of the Moon at Carrhae, Macrinus arranged that one of his equerries should stab him while he had dismounted to relieve himself.

At first Macrinus, who was now hailed as emperor, treated Julia with every respect; but as soon as he felt he could act with impunity, he ordered her to be gone from Antioch. At that, even

Julia could do no more. Already she was suffering from a cancer of the breast. She now starved herself to death.

So ended this great empress. Or rather so ended her worldly existence, because unlike any before her, she was able to hand on her life and its work to her sister. And it will be to her, to her daughters and her grandchildren that the remaining portion of this work will be dedicated.

CHAPTER XI

Towards the Sun

JULIA DOMNA WAS duly deified; her sister and her two nieces were to be her earthly heirs and executors. Moesa, Julia's younger sister, had spent the whole of her adult life in the public eye. Like Julia, she was a determined, dominating and devoted woman. She had married Julius Avitus, a Roman proconsul, who had successively administered Asia, Mesopotamia and Cyprus. Her married life took her from one government house to another; and it was only in 193, the year of Septimius' accession, that she was able to join her sister in Rome, and settle down to enjoy a lucrative widowhood, amid the pleasures and palaces and perquisites of Rome. She could now at last give her whole time and talents to her own enrichment and the advancement of her two daughters. Of these the elder was Suheima, a good Arabic name, a diminutive like so many others, meaning 'Little Arrow', or Soaemias in its western form. She married a Syrian from Apamea, between Emesa and Antioch, who had become a senator before his early death. Their one surviving son was Avitus Bassianus, later to be known as Elagabalus. Moesa's younger daughter was called Mammaea. She too married a Syrian, from Arqa, a cult-centre of Astarte fifteen miles north-east of Syrian Tripoli. Mammaea's husband only reached the rank of procurator, or imperial steward. He was of lower rank than his wife; but both Severus and Caracalla allowed her to retain her father's senatorial status. The only son of this marriage was Alexander. He was born at Arqa, and was only nine when he was sent back there, so that he always retained a Syrian cast of speech and manner of which he was very conscious. His father, too, died young.

The view from the Forum looking towards the Colosseum, by Canaletto

The Roman Forum

Macrinus was no soldier. Like his predecessor as praetorian prefect Papinian and his successor Ulpian, he was a jurist, but without any pretentions to the gifts of those two great men. At the outset of his reign, or usurpation (it lasted only fourteen months), Macrinus made a fatal mistake. Instead of separating the three widows, and relegating each of them to a different domicile as far distant as possible from their native land, he sent them all three, with the two boys, back to Emesa, the very hearth and centre of their influence and prestige, which they lost no time in exploiting. So recently the stars of Rome itself, they now shed their lustre throughout the Levant.

Hitherto this narrative has dealt with political and social aspects of Roman life, public and domestic. With the advent of the Syrians, the centre of gravity changes from the secular to the religious. Given the religious fervour and fecundity of the region, this is in reality no more than might be expected; but it was to have a profound and abiding influence not only on the fortunes of Rome but on the destinies of mankind.

As a first step towards the restoration of the family's primacy, and a return to Rome (for that and no less is what these spirited ladies were set on), Avitus Bassianus, now aged thirteen, became, like his forbears, high priest of the 'family' deity, the mountain-god, Ela-Gabal, who was venerated at Emesa in the form of a large black conical stone. This was said to have fallen from heaven, as it may well have done: other meteorites, including Cybele, the Great Mother, had achieved sanctity. The boy had thus taken the first essential step towards not only priestly precedence, but political eminence as well, thereby prefiguring, albeit unconsciously, the dual authority of the Papacy.

Macrinus, having committed one blunder, matched it with another. He was savage in punishment, and, reducing the privileges which the army had enjoyed under Caracalla, ordained that new recruits would be enlisted on the Septimian scale, a step which naturally perturbed the legionaries. Finally, instead of dispersing his army, which had been on active and inglorious service for four years, to their winter quarters, he kept them concentrated in Syria. As Abel puts it (II, 166) "It needed all Macrinus' mediocrity not to understand that the discontent of soldiers mobilised with no object at a point in Syria was bound to be disastrous to his cause." It was.

The IIIrd Gallic, 'Antoninus' (Caracalla's) Own', were

L

encamped near Emesa. The soldiers, having little to do, often came into the town, and for lack of any other occupation attended the ceremonies in the temple. They were captivated by the youthful pontiff, who was exceptionally handsome. His coins and busts do not display attractive features, indeed he resembles, in general facial structure, his cousin Caracalla; but his eyes are large and were probably lustrous, such as are not uncommon in both sexes in the Levant. Looking like Dionysus, he was arrayed in a trailing purple robe bordered with gold, and wore a crown encrusted with precious stones, which glanced and glittered in the sunlight, as he danced to the sound of a flute, attended by a train of lads and maidens of the country. It may seem strange that tough Roman soldiers should have been carried away by such an exhibition, until we reflect upon the conquests made in our own society by flashy adolescents and simpering footballers who by capers far less tasteful than those of Elagabalus reduce to hysteria devotees whose mental attainment is about that of the Roman peasant.

Moesa very sensibly took the demonstrations at their face value. The soldiers were longing for an Antoninus, to avenge their fallen emperor. Elagabalus (or Varius as he should properly be called) was an Antoninus, son of that same Caracalla, for both her daughters, she said, had formed part of the emperor's seraglio. Moesa also let it be known that she had at her disposal an enormous hoard of gold, amassed from her palace pickings augmented by gifts from satraps and princes to the sanctuary of the family god.

To the soldiers it seemed that a golden opportunity now lay open. Having thus rigged the dice, Moesa was hardy enough to risk all on a single throw. She made her way by night to the camp of the IIIrd, taking with her not only her grandchildren, but a wagon laden with gold. The gates were flung open, and the soldiers rapturously acclaimed those whom they regarded as the natural and legitimate heirs of their own Augusta, Julia Domna, and her son. On the next morning, 16th April 218, the whole army saluted Varius as emperor under the name of Antoninus. Macrinus sent against the embattled rebels a detachment of Moorish troops under the command of a certain Julian, a praetorian prefect. The troops, lured by the gold which sparkled from the enemy ramparts, went over to the insurgents. Julian was killed and his head, carefully wrapped up and sealed with

Julian's seal, was sent to Macrinus as though it were the head of Elagabalus. After one more forlorn hope had been routed, Macrinus met his end. The rebels, spurred on by the tears and reproaches of Moesa and Suheima both of whom appeared on the field of battle, were victorious. Once again arms had been vindicated, once again Syria had triumphed.

The now imperial party wintered at Nicomedia, in Bithynia, Dio's homeland, where the priest-emperor insisted on celebrating the outlandish rites of his religion. Moesa, who knew Rome as well as anybody, was disturbed by this; but her remonstrances only resulted in her headstrong grandson killing Gannys, a foster-child of Moesa, and reputed paramour of Suheima—a trustworthy and prudent adviser who had been largely responsible for his elevation. Elagabalus (it is better to call him that, though the *official* name was always M. Aurelius Antoninus: Roman writers, however, could not get even that name right and always called him Heliogabalus. *Helios* being the Greek word for sun, with which they knew he was connected) had inherited not only a physical resemblance to his late cousin, but also much of the cruelty inherent in the Severan strain. The fourteen-year-old sovereign wrote to the Senate calling himself son of Antoninus and grandson of Severus, with the self-conferred titles of *Pius Felix Invictus Augustus*, which curiously enough thenceforth became the official style of the Roman emperors. Moesa and Suheima were both made Augusta. In the summer of the year 219 Rome was dazzled by the arrival of this exotic boy-emperor, habited in garments of silk embroidered with purple and gold, wearing bracelets, a collar of gold and a crown in the shape of a tiara, enriched with pearls and gems. He was accompanied by the black aerolith. Once again Moesa begged him to wear woollen clothes, Roman-style, and not to affront the citizens of the Capital. Once again he paid no heed to her.

Elagabalus has for centuries been a synonym for all the deviations and eccentricities which the Victorians gathered up in the convenient dustpan of 'impurity'. For this there are two sufficient reasons, both very human. The first is that the sight of this boy from the Levant, bedizened like a Persian queen, parading through the hallowed courts of the Palatine attended by a giggling throng of epicene orientals, really did excite the disgust of the Romans, who had erroneously imagined that every known sexual attitude had for centuries been a part of their own conservative tradition.

No one likes being proved wrong. Elagabalus undoubtedly introduced new variations on the enigmatic theme; but it is also beyond question that he saw himself as a woman, and attempted a physical transformation which modern medicine might well have sanctioned and achieved. (Dio, LXXX, 16, 7; 17, 1.) It was the trauma of being left in the limbo between male and female that produced the ruinous results. Dio says that he would be ashamed to describe them, and then describes them at length. Many others have done so since. Which brings us to the second reason. People delight in sexual scandal. As it happens, Elagabalus was the last emperor to whom it could with either justification or safety be ascribed by contemporary writers. They therefore piled on every conceivable scrap of titillating gossip they could find. It was, they knew, their last fling.

Herodian admits that he was 'more effeminate than an honest woman would be'—again that Severan over-compensation for his unhappy condition. Mr Taunton, translating him in 1635, strikes a nice balance between Puritan reticence and what he knew the public wanted. So he published a little appendix—his only one —as follows:

His Apparell was extreme brave and gorgeous: yet he never wore one garment twice. His shoes were embellished with Diamonds and Oriental Pearles of the most Caracts. His seats were strewed with musk and amber, His Beds were covered with Cloth of Gold tissued on Purple, and imbossed with Gems of inestimable value. His Way was strewed with Filings of Gold & Silver. His Vessels, even of basest use, were of obryse Gold. His *Lamps* burned with precious Balms and Gums of India and Arabia. His *Fish-ponds* were filled with Rose-water. His *Ships* in his Theatrical Sea-fights floated in rivers of wine. His *Bathes*, most magnificently built, when he had once used them, were still pluckt down and new built. His Plate of refined massive Gold; but never served twice to his Table. His Rings and Jewels infinitely rich, yet never worn twice. His *concubines* numberless, but never lain with twice. Every Supper in his Court cost 1000 pounds sterling. When he lay near to the Sea, he would eat no Fish: when he was farthest in the Continent he would eat no Flesh. Whole Meals were furnisht with Tongues of Singing Birds, and Brains of rarest Creatures. All Europe, Asia and Africke, with the Islands adjacent; in a word the Globe of Earth and Sea (whereof he was *Lord Paramount*) was not able to fill this *Gulph*. In his Progress, he was attended by 600 Charriots fraught with Concubines, Catamites, and Pandars; for whom he built a Seraglio in his Court; where himself (in the habit of a Court-ezan) used to make solemn speeches to them, terming them his brave Fellow-Souldiers & Companions in Armes. (*What gallant Instructions he gave them I forbear to mention.*) He caused to be gathered in Rome ten thousand weight of Spiders, ten thousand Mice and a thousand polecats; which he exhibited to the Roman Peers and People in a publick Shew and Solemnity; professing that *now he perfectly understood how mighty a City Rome was.* Lastly (*to omit other more strange pranks*) he summoned a Parliament of Women to consult about *Tires, Fashions, Dresses, Tinctures* and the like weighty and important Affaires.

(If in the foregoing we seem to catch a sort of below-stairs echo of *Antony and Cleopatra*, we may recall that it was written only nineteen years after Shakespeare's death.)

The parliament of women was a harmless innovation, which was later revived by the emperor Aurelian. What was more indecorous was the introduction of his mother into the Senate, on his very first appearance there. "She was accommodated on the consuls' bench and there she took part in the drafting, that is to say she witnessed the drawing up of the Senate's decree." Or it may have been, and more probably was, his grandmother who was thus honoured. Both ladies were granted the right to coin.

Rome was practically ruled by the Syrian triad, for Mammaea was there, too, which as things turned out was fortunate not only for her but for Rome as well. Moesa realised that Elagabalus could not last long; she therefore arranged that he should adopt his cousin Alexander, her other grandson, who was only six years his junior.

The keenest and in the end fatal opposition to Elagabalus arose less from his personal behaviour, or even from his political and administrative vagaries—for the Roman machine of government was amazingly robust—than from his religious measures and aspirations. In a society where the very words '*novas res*', 'new things' were the accepted synonym for revolution, they were bound to lead to catastrophe. They did, and yet they are by far the most important element in his brief reign, and there were to have radical and abiding consequences, consequences which would endure as a generative force long after the miasma surrounding their author had been dispelled.

Roman religion, in so far as it existed, fell into two different categories. There was the official, public observance of the traditional liturgies. By the second century, this had become ossified into a web of taboos, held together by a tissue of superstition which it is simply not possible for a modern mind to grasp. At every step a Roman was tortured and tripped up by portents and omens, from earthquakes and thunderstorms, to withering trees, animals with two heads, or entrails of inauspicious shape or colour. This was not merely the surrogate of the poor and credulous for any spiritual apparatus; the upper ranks of intelligent society were enslaved by it. The pages of Dio, even of Tacitus, and of course the *Augustan History* are peppered with these infantile records of prodigies and premonitions. Only Herodian takes a more matter-of-fact line: "Oracles," he says, "are best credited when they are verified by events."

From early times men and women in Rome had realised that such cold, legalistic formulae, such thaumaturgic mumbo-jumbo, could not satisfy an intelligent and enquiring soul. More and more therefore they had turned to the east in their search for *salus*, health for the soul, and more and more had they found it in the religions of the Orient. Cybele, the Great Mother, had been the first to arrive, during the Second Punic War, in 204 BC. She was followed by a host of others, from Asia, Egypt and Persia. None of these deities claimed exclusive rights over the souls of men: you simply chose the one, or ones, that seemed to suit you best.

But gradually there had spread from Palestine a wholly new conception of religion. The Judaeo-Christian ethic *did* claim the sole right of direction, in return for which it would grant its adherents perpetual life, eternal *salus*, that is salvation. This faith guaranteed complete liberation from all lesser powers, from hobgoblins, omens and portents, from the trammels of flesh and mind alike. When St Paul wrote to his disciples in Philippi, "The truth has made you free," he meant precisely what he said.

Naturally this new conception of man and his nature and destiny aroused the sharpest opposition. It was *'novas res'* with a vengeance, and as such it must be and was resisted. By the beginning of the third century AD, it had made great conquests, despite periodical efforts to extirpate it.

Christians were first so called at Antioch, in the first century AD. It had been the centre of the early Church. It was natural therefore that when the great city was also the abode of the imperial Court, the princesses should have had some contact, however remote, with the new Faith. In fact, they came to know it at first hand. Eusebius the Church Historian of the fourth century tells us that Mammaea "a religious woman if ever there was one" sent a military escort to bring to her side the great Origen himself. Origen was a master spirit. His attitude to Holy Writ is amazingly modern. At the outset of his Sixfold Version of the Old Testament he inveighs against a 'Fundamentalist' approach to the Bible. "What man of sense," he writes, "will suppose that the first and second and third day, and the evening and the morning, existed without sun and moon and stars? Or that God walked in the garden in the evening and that Adam hid himself under a tree? Or that the Devil took Jesus into a high mountain from which he could see the kingdom of the Persians, and Scythians, and Indians?" Such passages are valuable only for their spiritual meaning. Origen was equally frank about the discrepancies between the Synoptic Gospels: like the Old Testament, they are simply media through which a higher meaning, the divine Gospel, is expressed. The Fourth Gospel is a symbolic exposition.

At the same time, Origen made it quite clear that he was utterly opposed to the secular, pagan, state.

It was at this moment of balance, when, from the Christian point of view, "night was almost at odds with morning, which is which," that the Syrians came to dominate Rome. Elagabalus was the first emperor ever to demand religious uniformity. And he demanded it in the guise of acceptance of a monotheism, that of the worship of the Sun.

There was to be no more tolerance, or as it seemed to him, indifference. All men and the Roman state were to worship one supreme god. This in itself was a remarkable conception for a fifteen-year-old boy to entertain.

Sun-worship was no stranger to Rome. The importation of Egyptian obelisks, symbols of the sun's rays, has already been mentioned. Before the second battle of Cremona, in AD 69,

Tacitus tells us (*Histories*, III, 24) that the troops who had served in Syria, saluted the sun on rising, as they had learned to do in Syria. Sun-worship then was established as respectable—in its Roman guise. But to have it promoted, nay enforced, by an eccentric boy, a circumcised Syrian who abstained from pork (a staple food of the Roman populace), who claimed to be the Sun's High Priest, that was too much, even without his other eccentricities, including his four or five wives, who by no means prevented him from indulgence in extra-marital excesses in a depraved spirit of give and take.

Moesa, alas, was right. Elagabalus twice tried to have Alexander killed. This goaded the praetorians to action, probably with Moesa's connivance. On 11th March 222, Elagabalus and his mother were slaughtered in the palace, and their headless corpses dishonoured. The emperor's was flung into the Tiber.

It is by no means easy to form a just estimate of the character and behaviour of Elagabalus. Without doubt, his heredity disposed him to cruelty and lechery—even his mother's example was deplorable. In addition he was headstrong and vain, especially in what our Mr Taunton calls his 'hiddy-giddy veneration' of his god. Not all of this can be excused by his psychopathic condition. On the other hand, judged by the touchstone of durability, the achievement of this adolescent is outstanding, for it was he who dared to advance monotheism to sovereign spiritual status. His methods were wrong and foolish; but in this respect his aims were wholly laudable, and it was those aims that were to reach their target, and to be acknowledged, when his follies were forgotten.

Alexander succeeded without opposition. It was Moesa's last *coup*: she died the next year (223), her great work fully accomplished.

Once again, we may turn to Balsdon for her epitaph:

Her brave and venturesome life had brought its disappointments. But at the end she could afford to reflect on the success with which, time and again, she had foreseen danger and had forestalled it. Her courage she shared with the other women of the family, her sister and her two daughters. Her death, in its surprising peacefuless, was her own. She was not murdered, as both her daughters were murdered. She had not, like her sister, to take her own life.

Moesa had never been the consort of an emperor, but she had proved herself to be a great empress.

Mammaea was determined to perpetuate the family influence; but she lacked the address, and be it added, the integrity, of her mother. She was duly hailed as 'Mother of Augustus and the Camps'. She was excluded from the Senate, but sixteen members of the House were chosen to be her coadjutors in what was in effect a council of regency, the new emperor being but thirteen and a half years old. This arrangement safeguarded Alexander, but it encouraged his mother to ever more overweaning arrogance. She wrecked her son's marriage, and in the end, by her ill-timed parsimony and pro-Levantine favouritism brought about the death of both Alexander and herself at the hands of the troops, late in March in the year 235. Alexander was twenty-five, and had ruled for less than thirteen years.

Our sources hardly help us with Alexander's reign. Herodian treats of him, but, being an easterner, is almost wholly concerned with his activities in the never-ending tussles with the Persians. Dio records his accession, but then excuses himself from a more detailed account on the ground that he 'was seldom in Rome'. And yet he was consul with Alexander in 229: he could certainly have told us much more had he wished to do so. Thus, we are almost wholly dependent on the *Augustan History*. For some reason the author of Alexander's *Life*, whoever he may have been, chose this emperor to represent the 'model ruler' no doubt as prefiguring Constantine, to whom the *Life* is dedicated. In such eulogies, however oblique, "a man is not on oath". Alexander receives more space than any other emperor or usurper in the entire collection: where Elagabalus was all black, Alexander is all white. Some of the incidents in the narrative are demonstrably false, which undermines our faith in the work as a whole.

It is in the spiritual sphere that the reign of Alexander is of particular interest. Alexander was simple in his tastes, modest and chaste. He did his best to purge Roman society. Only women of unblemished repute were received at court, from which eunuchs were banished and degraded to the status of slaves. Women of ill fame were rounded up and consigned to the public stews. The taxes levied on pimps and prostitutes of both sexes were paid into a special fund, which was devoted to the repair of ancient monuments. It is to this curious source of revenue that we owe in part the preservation of the theatre of Marcellus and the Colosseum. Catamites were deported. Alexander wanted to abolish male prostitution altogether, but was dissuaded on the ground that "such a prohibition would merely convert an evil recognised by the state into a vice practised in private"—an argument which has been advanced in a similar context in more recent ages. It remained for another Syrian, Philip the Arab, to disestablish this perversion.

So good, so austere a ruler, of such humane and gentle tendencies, might well be expected to show tolerance to the Christians. In fact he went further, he took an active interest in their doctrine. He often quoted their precepts, as well as those of the Jews. He placed statues of Christ and Abraham in his private chapel, alongside those of Orpheus and Apollonius of Tyana. He would have liked to build a temple to Christ. He had the Golden Rule engraved on his palace and on public buildings, and had a herald recite it at the punishment of malefactors. He courted leading Christians. Julius Africanus, a Christian historian, was invited to Rome, and founded a library there. Mammaea's patronage of Origen has been mentioned. St Hippolytus of Rome, whose almost contemporary statue, with a table for finding the date of Easter on his chair, now adorns the new galleries of the Vatican Museum, dedicated a treatise on the Resurrection to her.

The reign of Alexander, however much of its recorded details we may reject or accept, does bring us to an age when Christianity was tolerated. Tolerated yes, but no more. Toleration implies compromise, and Christianity could not compromise. No great cause has ever been vindicated by compromise. The Church had still to undergo the most awful tribulation it had ever undergone, or was ever to undergo until the twentieth century, nothing less than a brutal and determined effort to extinguish it altogether. But it is largely to the Syrian dynasty, led by its resolute ladies, that we must accord the merit of having established an environment in which the soldiers of the Faith could enter on the struggle with confidence in their ultimate victory.

Epilogue

HERE ENDS THE tale, and that for two reasons. The first is that after the death of Alexander Severus the Empire became the prey of a welter of successive dynasts, whose careers and actions are hardly worth recording, and but scrappily recorded; and of whose wives we know next to nothing. We do not know even what became of Alexander's second wife, Memmia. (His first, who reproached him for being too affable, was banished by his mother's contrivance and her father killed.) The flickering light of the *Augustan History* goes out in 244, and is rekindled only in 253 for just one more blood-thirsty generation.

The second reason is that the revolution, or reformation, inaugurated by the Syrians remains in abeyance—but only in abeyance—until the emergence of the last great 'Roman' emperors, Aurelian, in 270. He came from Illyria, modern Jugoslavia, but during his short reign of five years he did much to re-establish Rome. He recognised the inevitable, and withdrew Rome's physical bulwark from the Tyne to the Tiber, as the russet girdle of his Wall still attests. He is best known for his defeat of Zenobia, queen of Palmyra, a second Julia Domna as Abel calls her. Like Zenobia Aurelian was an ardent devotee of the Unconquered Sun. His mother is said to have been a priestess of the solar cult, and Aurelian himself built and endowed a temple of the Sun in Rome. Coins of his minting bear the inscription *Sol Dominus Imperii Romani*—'Sun Lord of the Roman Empire', as clear a proclamation of the faith of which he was to be the Defender as could possibly be made.

Diocletian, in the twenty years following 284, transformed the old Empire into an eastern, absolute monarchy; but he also

paved the way for the transference of the seat of supreme spiritual
and temporal power from Rome to Byzantium, and so to the
inauguration of a régime which was to last for more than a
millennium. Constantine like Aurelian had been brought up to
revere the Unconquered Sun; but he was to take the ultimate
step along the way which had been opened by the Syrians: he
adopted monotheism in its Christian form.

This was the ultimate achievement of the ultimate Caesars'
wives. How strangely, disjointedly, it had come to pass. Twenty-
four emperors had been cherished, betrayed or killed by nearly
thirty women, not a few of whom had met their ends at their
husbands' hands. How few, how lamentably few, of these women
had produced an heir begotten by their emperors, and of those
heirs how even fewer had been anything but a curse. Titus,
Domitian, Commodus, Caracalla (Geta can hardly be included)—
that is the sole tale: four out of a possible minimum of twenty-
four, and of that quartet Titus alone is praiseworthy. What a
dolorous, damning record.

> Are God and Nature then at strife,
>   That Nature lends such evil dreams?
>   So careful of the type she seems,
> So careless of the single life.

Already in 1850 Alfred Tennyson was faced with the perpetual
problem. We, in our generation, are faced with it more alarm-
ingly and acutely than ever, because Nature in terms both of time
and of space, aided by archaeology and astrophysics, has vastly
expanded her realm, and the individual, the 'single life', finds it
harder than ever to maintain its identity.

This really was the cardinal problem of antiquity as well—the
pathetic proclamation of an 'aeternitas' which was never achieved.
How utterly careless of the 'single life' Roman society in all its
manifestations was—that is one of the most depressing features
of Rome's recorded history.

That it fell to Caesars' wives, if to only a few of them, to
alleviate this brutality, and to point the way to an age in which
the single life would be respected, in which eternity would for so
many become a reality, is their just reward. In this at least those
of them who thus strove are indeed above suspicion, and above
all that we can bestow upon them in the way of posthumous pity
and gratitude.

Racine: passages from *Britannicus* and *Bérénice*

(See pages 72, 81 and 105)

From *Britannicus*
Agrippina's appeal to Nero, Act IV, Scene II.

AGRIPPINE, s'asseyant
Approchez-vous, Néron, et prenez votre place.
On veut sur vos soupçons que je vous satisfasse.
J'ignore de quel crime on a pu me noircir :
De tous ceux que j'ai faits je vais vous éclaircir.
 Vous régnez : vous savez combien votre naissance
Entre l'empire et vous avait mis de distance.
Les droits de mes aïeux, que Rome a consacrés,
Étaient même sans moi d'inutiles degrés.
Quand de Britannicus la mère condamnée
Laissa de Claudius disputer l'hyménée,
Parmi tant de beautés qui briguèrent son choix,
Qui de ses affranchis mendièrent les voix,
Je souhaitai son lit, dans la seule pensée
De vous laisser au trône où je serais placée.
Je fléchis mon orgueil ; j'allai prier Pallas.
Son maître, chaque jour caressé dans mes bras,
Prit insensiblement dans les yeux de sa nièce
L'amour où je voulais amener sa tendresse.
Mais ce lien du sang qui nous joignait tous deux
Écartait Claudius d'un lit incestueux :
Il n'osait épouser la fille de son frère.
Le sénat fut séduit : une loi moins sévère

Mit Claude dans mon lit, et Rome à mes genoux.
C'était beaucoup pour moi, ce n'était rien pour vous.
    Je vous fis sur mes pas entrer dans sa famille;
Je vous nommai son gendre, et vous donnais sa fille:
Silanus, qui l'aimait, s'en vit abandonné,
Et marqua de son sang ce jour infortuné.
Ce n'était rien encore. Eussiez-vous pu prétendre
Qu'un jour Claude à son fils pût préférer son gendre?
De ce même Pallas j'implorai le secours:
Claude vous adopta, vaincu par ses discours,
Vous appela Néron; et du pouvoir suprême.
Voulut avant le temps, vois faire part lui-même.
C'est alors que chacun, rappelant le passé,
Découvrit mon dessein déjà trop avancé:
Que de Britannicus la disgrâce future
Des amis de son père excita le murmure.
Mes promesses aux uns éblouirent les yeux;
L'exil me délivra des plus séditieux;
Claude même, lassé de ma plainte éternelle,
Éloigna de son fils tous ceux de qui le zèle,
Engagé dès longtemps à suivre son destin,
Pouvait du trône encor lui rouvrir le chemin.
Je fis plus: je choisis moi-même dans ma suite
Ceux à qui je voulais qu'on livrât sa conduite;
J'eus soin de vois nommer, par un contraire choix,
Des gouverneurs que Rome honorait de sa voix;
Je fus sourde à la brigue, et crus la renommée;
J'appelai de l'exil, je tirai de l'armée,
Et ce même Sénèque, et ce même Burrhus,
Qui depuis . . . Rome alors estimait leurs vertus.
De Claude en même temps épuisant les richesses,
Ma main, sous votre nom, répandait ses largesses;
Les spectacles, les dons, invincibles appas,
Vous attiraient les cœurs du peuple et des soldats,
Qui d'ailleurs, réveillant leur tendresse première,
Favorisaient en vous Germanicus mon père.
    Cependant Claudius penchait vers son déclin.
Ses yeux, longtemps fermés, s'ouvrirent à la fin:
Il connut son erreur. Occupé de sa crainte,
Il laissa pour son fils échapper quelque plainte,
Et voulut, mais trop tard, assembler ses amis.
Ses gardes, son palais, son lit m'étaient soumis.
Je lui laissai sans fruit consumer sa tendresse;
Des ses derniers soupirs je me rendis maîtresse:
Mes soins, en apparence, épargnant ses douleurs,

De son fils, en mourant, lui cachèrent les pleurs.
Il mourut. Mille bruits en courent à ma honte.
J'arrêtai de sa mort la nouvelle trop prompte;
Et tandis que Burrhus allait secrètement
De l'armée en vos mains exiger le serment,
Que vous marchiez au camp, conduit sous mes auspices,
Dans Rome les autels fumaient de sacrifices;
Par mes ordres trompeurs tout le peuple excité
Du prince déjà mort demandait la santé.
Enfin, des légions l'entière obéissance
Ayant de votre empire affermi la puissance,
On vit Claude; et le peuple, étonné de son sort,
Apprit en même temps votre règne et sa mort.
   C'est le sincère aveu que je voulais vous faire:
Voilà tous mes forfaits. En voici le salaire:
   Du fruit de tant de soins à peine jouissant
En avez-vous six mois paru reconnaissant,
Que, lassé d'un respect qui vous gênait peut-être,
Vous avez affecté de ne me plus connaître.
J'ai vu Burrhus, Sénèque, aigrissant vos soupçons,
De l'infidélité vous tracer des leçons,
Ravis d'être vaincus dans leur propre science.
J'ai vu favorisés de votre confiance
Othon, Sénécion, jeunes voluptueux,
Et de tous vos plaisirs flatteurs respectueux;
Et lorsque, vos mépris excitant mes murmures,
Je vous ai demandé raison de tant d'injures,
(Seul recours d'un ingrat qui se voit confondu)
Par de nouveaux affronts vous m'avez répondu.
Aujourd'hui je promets Junie à votre frère;
Ils se flattent tous deux du choix de votre mère:
Que faites-vous? Junie, enlevée à la cour,
Devient en une nuit l'objet de votre amour;
Je vois de votre cœur Octavie effacée,
Prête à sortir du lit où je l'avais placée;
Je vois Pallas banni, votre frère arrêté;
Vous attentez enfin jusqu'à ma liberté:
Burrhus ose sur moi porter ses mains hardies.
Et lorsque, convaincu de tant de perfidies,
Vous deviez ne me voir que pour les expier,
C'est vous qui m'ordonnez de me justifier!

From *Britannicus*
The Denunciation, Act V, Scene VI

NÉRON, voyant Agrippine,

Dieux!

AGRIPPINE

Arrêtez Néron; j'ai deux mots à vous dire. Britannicus est mort;
je reconnais les coups; Je connais l'assassin.

NÉRON

Et qui, Madame?

AGRIPPINE

Vous.

From *Bérénice*
Bérénice's farewell, Act IV, Scene V

Je n'écoute plus rien: et, pour jamais, adieu . . .
Pour jamais! Ah! seigneur! songez-vous en vous-même
Combien ce mot cruel est affreux quand on aime?
Dans un mois, dans un an, comment souffrirons-nous,
Seigneur, que tant de mers me séparent de vous;
Que le jour recommence, et que le jour finisse,
Sans que jamais Titus puisse voir Bérénice,
Sans que, de tout le jour, je puisse voir Titus?
Mais quelle est mon erreur, et que de soins perdus!
L'ingrat, de mon départ consolé par avance,
Daignera-t-il compter les jours de mon absence?
Ces jours si longs pour moi lui sembleront trop courts.

Ancient Poisons

I am indebted to Dr P. C. H. Newbold of the Cambridge University Medical School for the following note:

Theophrastus, the pupil of Aristotle, discussed poisons in a treatise *perì tōn daketon kaì bletikon* (Loeb) in or about the year 300 BC. Attalus II, Philometer, of Pergamum was a renowned poisoner of the second century BC who makes Nero look like an innocent apprentice. Mithradates of Pontus (first century BC) is said to have immunised himself against poison, like Agrippina in a later age, by taking small doses of poisons over a long period. This started the interesting development of the theriac (antidote). According to Lucan (*Pharsalia*, VI, 438 seq.) the use of poisons was introduced into Rome in the first century BC from Thessaly, the traditional home of barbaric rites and witchcraft. By the first century AD, poisoning had become common in Rome. Juvenal specifies that aconite was used by mothers to remove children whose inheritances they coveted. Before the invention of firearms poison was the safest method of killing at a distance; nor before the development of medico-legal pathology was the criminal likely to be detected. There was nevertheless a special court for poison cases at Rome.

Early European writers on poisons and remedies were Petrus de Albano, *De venenis eorumque remediis*, Venice, 1473; and Baccuis *De venenis et antidotis*, Rome, 1586. Both these works imply that poisoning was a hazard to be guarded against in Renaissance Italy.

The emperors used poison quite openly on occasion. At other times they did feel that it would be desirable that the deaths of their victims should appear to be natural, and two such murders are described in this book, those of the emperor Claudius and of his son Britannicus. In each case a professional poisoner, Locusta, a woman of Gaul, was employed. (See *Locuste et Néron* in *La Chronique Médicale*, XX, 214–1913.)

The death of Claudius, as the author suggests, could easily have been contrived by the simple method of substituting a poisonous fungus for a genuine mushroom. Accidental death from this cause, due to ignorance or carelessness, still occurs in Italy. Death is mainly caused by *Amanita phalloides*, which can easily be confused with *Boletus edulis*, to which as we know from Seneca's *Apokolokyntosis* Claudius was excessively partial. Claudius' case is discussed by Cabarès et Nass in *Poisons et Sortilèges*, p. 126, Paris, Plon-Nourrit, 1903.

For the death of Britannicus we may turn to M. Littré in *Gazette Hebdomadaire de Médécine et de Chirurgerie*, Paris, 1853, I(8), 101–106 and 133–137. Seneca tells us that artists in poisons could prepare fatal brews without either taste or smell. Arrian warns a master not to be too hard on a slave who serves water too hot or too cold. This was the setting for the murder of Britannicus. The slave brought the prince too hot a draught. He asked for it to be cooled. The cup had already been tested for poison, and found innocuous. Into it the fatal additive was now poured.

The only poison that fits the recorded symptoms is prussic acid. Features of prussic acid poisoning are:

> Sudden collapse
> Convulsions and muscle-twitching
> Skin eruptions
> Unconsciousness
> Death from respiratory failure.

This was precisely the death-syndrome of Britannicus.

The natural sources of prussic acid are the seeds of fruits of the *prunus* family—almond, apricot, cherry, choke cherry, wild cherry and peach. (To which in our own age we can add Japanese plum, loquat, tapioca plant and hydrangea.) All contain glycosides from which cyanide can be made. The seeds are first crushed, and then the extract is concentrated.

Arsenic, obtained from copper, was available to ancient poisoners, but they seem to have favoured the vegetable varieties. Pliny mentions yew, and other sources record henbane, hemlock and atropine.

P. C. H. NEWBOLD

The Roman Emperors and their Wives
27 BC–AD 235

	BC	
27	Augustus	1. Clodia
		2. Scribonia
		3. Livia
	AD	
14	Tiberius	1. Vipsania Agrippina
		2. Julia
37	Gaius (Caligula)*	4. Milonia Caesonia
41	Claudius*	3. Valeria Messalina
		4. Julia Agrippina
54	Nero	1. Octavia
		2. Poppaea Sabina
		3. Statilia Messalina
68	Galba	
	Otho	Poppaea Sabina (before Nero)
69	Vitellius	Galeria Fundana
	Vespasian	1. Flavia Domitilla
		2. Antonia Caenis
79	Titus	(Berenice)
81	Domitian	1. Domitia
		2. Julia
96	Nerva	
98	Trajan	Pompeia Plotina
117	Hadrian	Vibia Sabina
138	Antoninus Pius	Faustina I
161	Marcus Aurelius	Faustina II
180	Commodus	Crispina
	Pertinax	Titiana
193	Didius Julianus	
	Septimius Severus	Julia Domna
211	Caracalla	Fulvia
217	Macrinus	
218	Elagabalus	1. Julia Cornelia
		2. Julia Aquilia
		3. Annia Aurelia
222	Severus Alexander	

* Gaius had three previous wives, and Claudius two, not mentioned in this book.

THE CLAUDIANS

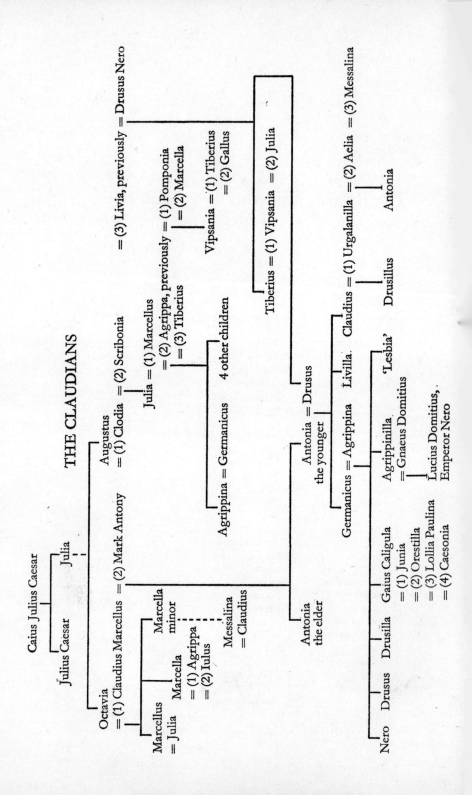

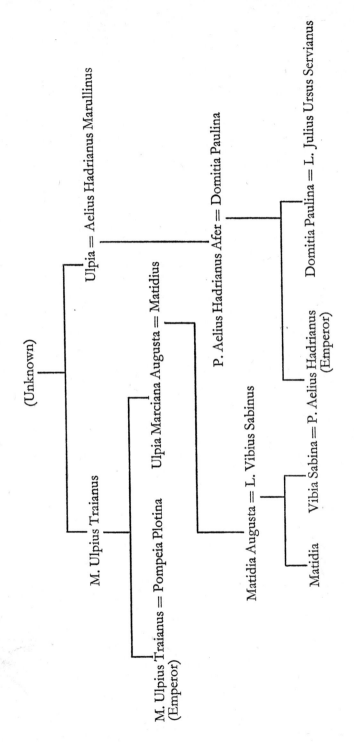

HADRIAN AND HIS ANCESTORS

(Unknown)

Ulpia = Aelius Hadrianus Marullinus

M. Ulpius Traianus

M. Ulpius Traianus = Pompeia Plotina
(Emperor)

Ulpia Marciana Augusta = Matidius

P. Aelius Hadrianus Afer = Domitia Paulina

Matidia Augusta = L. Vibius Sabinus

Matidia

Vibia Sabina = P. Aelius Hadrianus
(Emperor)

Domitia Paulina = L. Julius Ursus Servianus

THE SYRIANS

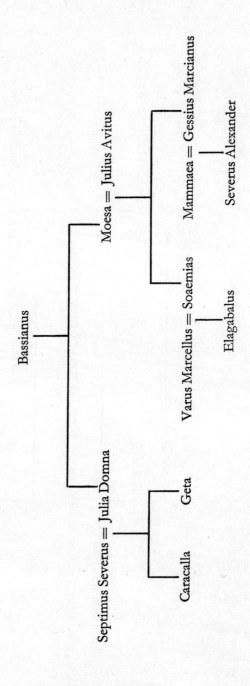

Septimus Severus = Julia Domna

Bassianus

Moesa = Julius Avitus

Caracalla

Geta

Varus Marcellus = Soaemias

Mammaea = Gessius Marcianus

Elagabalus

Severus Alexander

Acknowledgements

So far as is known, the first attempt in English to treat of the wives of the Roman emperors was a work called: *The Roman Empresses; or, The History of the Lives and Secret Intrigues of the Wives of the Twelve Caesars, with historical and critical notes.* This was translated by the Hon. Bysse Molesworth from the French original of Jacques Roergas de Serviez which appeared in 1720, and was published by R. Dodsley in Pall Mall in 1752. The book was reprinted in a limited edition of 1,000 copies by the Walpole Press in 1899.

There is no notice of Bysse Molesworth in the *Dictionary of National Biography*, nor does he appear to have written anything except this one book. I am indebted to the present Lord Molesworth for the following information about him. The Hon. Bysse Molesworth was the seventh son of the first viscount, and he married in 1731 Elizabeth, sister of John, first Lord Mount-Florence and widow of Edward Archdale Esq, of Castle Archdale, Co. Fermanagh. He died in 1779 leaving issue. He and his wife resided at Brachestown, Swords, Co. Dublin. Their descendants are still living. It has not been possible to discover any literary or other memorials of him.

In the preparation of the present essay I have received help from many sources. Once again I thank my old friends, the Revd. Joseph Crehan, S.J., and the Revd. Gervase Mathew, O.P., for their unstinted bestowal of scholarship and counsel. I also wish to thank Professor Denis Arnold of Nottingham University for information regarding Monteverdi and *L'Incoronazione di Poppaea*; the Archivisiste-Bibliothécaire of the Comédie Française for statistics regarding Racine's *Britannicus* and *Bérénice*; Dr Michael Grant for permission to quote from his translation of the *Annals* of Tacitus in the Penguin Classics; and the publishers of the Loeb Classical Library for similar courtesy in respect of their editions of Suetonius, Dio Cassius and the *Augustan History*. I must also once again record my grateful reliance on the works of two great scholars now alas, dead: Franz Cumont (*Les Réligions Paiennes dans l'Empire Romain*) and the Revd. F.-M. Abel, O.P. (*Histoire de la Palestine depuis la conquête d'Alexandre jusqu'à l'Invasion Arabe*). They are the indispensible guides to even the most cursory investigation of religious developments in the Roman Empire.

Very specially I thank Dr J. P. V. D. Balsdon for most generously allowing me to make extensive use of his scholarly and delightful *Roman Women*. Finally I thank Dr Peter Newbold for furnishing a note on ancient poisons. Parts of the text, chiefly in the later chapters, have appeared in a different context in books of my own: *The Later Herods, Hadrian* and *Caesars and Saints*.

Index